Press On

RICKIA BROWN

DEDICATION

I dedicate this book to God. God, I thank you for choosing me. Although I may not have understood some of the things that I have went through, I now understand why. I thank you for being the co-author of this book. I thank you for placing the spirit of diligence in my heart to be able to focus and execute this project. I thank you for always being there and most recently forcing me to silence myself to be able to finally hear your voice. In life I have struggled with my emotions by keeping everything bottled in. It is a breath of fresh air to finally be able to express my emotions and help others in the process. I thank you for my testimony that I was unable to comprehend initially. You now have my full attention and I simply thank you in advance for the hearts, minds, and spirits that this book touches. Please forgive me for not trusting or turning to you when I should have. I feel honored to be of your service. Thank you God for giving me the voice to propel my story in only a way that I can. I pray that my story helps and changes the lives and perspective of others.

CONTENTS

ACKNOWLEDGMENTS

I thank my amazing husband Brandon who has been very supportive of me telling my story with the good, the bad and the ugly. Thank you for always being my number one fan and always believing in me. I thank my two beautiful children Marley B. and Sélah Chase for being my greatest and latest inspirations. You two push me to #presson even in times when I don't feel or have not felt like it. I also want to thank my clients for inspiring me to write my book. I have told many of you my experiences and my story, and many times have had you in tears whether it was from laughing or genuinely being happy for me.

1 CONSULTATION
LET ME TELL YOU WHAT HAS BEEN GOING ON

This book is straight "shop talk". In hair salons and barber shops there is absolutely no conversation off limits. We share our deepest secrets in the chair of our hairstylist and barbers. We don't feel judged in their chairs. There is no order to our conversations in "shop talk". One minute we could be talking about Real Housewives, the next we could be talking about a toxic relationship. Shop talk has no flow, it's free formed. Never look for order in "shop talk", there is none in the shop, and there is none in this book. Shop talk doesn't always go in chronological order of events, so don't look for that either. I have been both the client and the hairstylist. 98% of the time I am the hairstylist. I hold the key to some of your deepest secrets. Before you leave my chair you will leave with something! You may leave with a hug, words of encouragement, something inspiring, or whatever other positive thing you could think of. I make sure that you leave full. Me? Well, many days I have left empty. I have poured so much into others

1

and have drained myself in the process. I have issues just like you, I just mask them. That's my job, to be a master at masking my emotions. Do you know how hard that is? Do you know what it is like to carry so much weight in with you to work and have to leave it at the door, only to pick it back up when you leave? I have not only taken on my issues, but I have taken on my client's issues as well. I have heard some things from clients that have left me crying and hugging them in the middle of their appointment. Days like that I have left crying about my issues AND theirs. I am one weight when I come in, and a different weight when I leave. I gain weight as a hairstylist. Sometimes I just want to be that client in the chair that can let out my cries. Prepare yourself for my position. You are now the hairstylist that listens and I am now the client that vents. Have your shoulder ready for me to cry on, your ear open for me to vent to, your eyes clear to see what I have been through, and make sure your chair is sturdy for me because I am about to take you for a ride. Many of you have heard pieces of my story, I always make my long story short. Today, the short story is long. *__Takes a deep breath in and exhales slowly__* Let the "shop talk" begin!

I was in a relationship with now husband Brandon for 11 years before I decided that I needed to leave him. During the 11 years, we were engaged for 5 years, had two children, moved into our fourth place together, and talked about marriage but it just never happened. Women tend to mature at a much faster rate than men, and sometimes that causes a big growth spurt that requires that woman to "grow" on without that man. Growth is what we both needed for our story. I got to the point where I was just tired of putting on my mask as a hairstylist. I was tired of putting clients under the dryer while I stepped to the end of the hallway, (where the trash was) and cried my eyes out. This had become my weekly routine. I would shampoo a client and say, "I'll be right back, I have to use the bathroom". As I ran past the bathroom I would find "my corner" right by the trash, and cry and pray and pray and cry. You know how you cry and you get that sleepy yawn and something about that yawn just makes you feel a little better? That was the cry I was managing in the hall on a weekly basis.

People always relate cheating to why a person leaves a relationship. Trust me, there are tons of other reasons why people finally decide they have had enough. For me, I was just tired of feeling alone. What is the point of being in a relationship, having a nice place together, kids and always being there alone? During the 11 years I realized you can't change a man. A man is going to change when he is ready to change. In the meantime what you can do is change you. The nights of being up all night, blowing up his phone, sitting up crying, and trying to figure out why his friends came before his family was OVER. The best relationship advice I can give is, "girl go to sleep". At the end of the day when a man is out having fun and living life, he is going to sleep good at night and you should do the same. Baby I mastered giving it to God and going to sleep.

NOW! This is how I intended to start this book. Just with a brief of the relationship Brandon and I had. During this writing process I am fasting every Tuesday and Wednesday, these are my writing days. Today I got confirmation that I needed to be VERY transparent. I have to be obedient to what God is requesting me to do. This is my therapy and maybe it should not be filtered for if it is, it will not help me or help someone else to its fullest potential. I asked God for confirmation on what I should do and I just got it through my good girlfriend Amy. She told me that everyone couldn't relate to a fairytale ending. People need to know that my "fairytale wedding" did not come by way of the best experiences. People need to know my truths. Truth is, my life hasn't been perfect. I have struggled with so many things in my life that have contributed to me being emotionally dysfunctional.

Truth is Brandon and I have had the best of ups and the worst of downs. My main reason for leaving him was for his disrespect over and over again towards me. I have been called every b!tch in the book, been disrespected in public and in private, and I have been embarrassed and humiliated to unexplainable depths. It wasn't until I had kids that I realized that some of the trauma that I had dealt with was not ok, and they needed to see better examples of what a healthy relationship should look like. I have always been a very private person, completely opposite of Brandon. When we would have issues I would vent to one if not all of my three friends; Tyeisha, Ashley and Shawnise. Each of these friends represents a certain level of tolerance for the things that I was going through.

I know that with Tyeisha I could only tell her the surface of things. Tye is my friend that has little to no tolerance. Tye is a libra. If I call her, I better not cry. Tye is not a crier. Tye takes a situation for what it is and moves on. You will never be able to hold Tye up for the 11 years that Brandon was able to hold me up. I learned what I could only afford to tell Tye through trial and error. One day, I believe we were about maybe 22 or 23 and I was venting to Tye about Brandon not answering the phone. I cannot clearly remember all of the details of what it was about, but I do remember crying really hard and thinking I could cry about him on her shoulders. That is the day I learned, you don't cry on Tye's shoulders about a man! She immediately said, "B##CH I KNOW YOU ARE NOT CRYING"! I ended up feeling so stupid and embarrassed, I mean it to the upmost! From that point, I realized that I could only call and vent to Tye when it was a "pull up" situation. She is the "pull up" friend. She is going to help pull you up off the ground and pull up on a location. I would call her when Brandon wouldn't come home and say, "Girl he said he fell asleep on the couch at his brother's house". She would get so quiet and say, "Rickia you really believe that"? I would say "yeah". Her answer would be, "Rickia get the f**k out of here". Do yall remember the scene on "Waiting to Exhale" when the guy was stealing from Robin and Savannah told her that he took the money? I was Robin, "you think so"? Tye was Savannah, her reaction was like "girl if you don't get off my phone". LOL. I hate to admit it, but I have been the naïve/lingering friend. Many things went over my head. Tye is the type that she doesn't need proof beyond reasonable doubt like me. All she needs is for a dude to come up with a lame excuse one time and that's how she calculates the BS. When we were in college and she and her boyfriend broke up, she listened to Ushers "Let it Burn" cd everyday. She never picked up the phone to call him. It was like a thug mourning. Sometimes she would have her shades on when I would walk in her room with her mourning uniform. The mourning uniform was a tie-dyed Ben and Jerry's shirt, some gray sweat pants and her faux locs. I swear this went on for like a month straight. I hated that Usher CD because of her. When she was done mourning she kept it moving as if nothing ever happened. If I could be more like Tye that would be the part of her that I would love to have, the ability not to let a man hold her up or waste her time. Over the 11 years that Brandon and I were together Tye would flat out say, "Brandon's time would have BEEN up Rickia if that was me". Having a family OR not Tye is that friend that would suggest you to flat out LEAVE if you were not being treated right. PERIOD! Tye is the friend we need for a wake up call. Tye gives advice that gives you a reality check that reminds you of who you are and things that you should not tolerate. She is not going to tiptoe over your feelings. In the movie "Girls Trip", she is Dina. She is just going to pull the wax right off, it's going to burn but it's going to be quick and straight to the point.

Ashley. She is my listening friend. I can run to Ashley crying and not be judged. Ashley is a cancer. Go figure. LOL. Getting answers from her though? Nope, Ashley doesn't give answers. I would cry and call Ashley and tell her about Brandon calling me a "b##ch", or give her the spill on how I went through his phone and saw some questionable things. Her response is always so predictable and simple; she takes a deep breath and says, "Uh I don't know Rickia, I don't know". Sometimes she may say, "I mean I can't say for sure because I wasn't there so I don't know". She is the safe friend. She plays every corner safe. She is very careful with her wording of advice. You would never be able to go to someone and say that Ashley said anything that she did not say. Ashley is very organized and could probably vouch for anything she has ever said in her life. She never suggested that I leave Brandon. Her advice never really helped me because she didn't give too much of it. She was more of a listener. Her words of advice would validate the battles of my thoughts in my own mind; "Yeah I wasn't there, I can't say for sure". Ashley is my mysterious friend. I never know whom or if she is dating, or what is really going on in her private life. I always joke with her and say she is a millionaire and we don't know. Ashley doesn't discuss finances and relationships. LOL. Sometimes we need that friend that would just listen. Talking to Ashley is almost like talking to a therapist. It's like you get to check in, pour your heart out and not feel pressured to make a decision. I could not even tell you how Ashley would react to some of the things that I have been through because she is so private. She could be going through a divorce right now and meanwhile I did not even know she was married. That is Ashley, very private. Very CIA-ish. LOL.

With Shawnise, you are going to get a little of Tye and a little of
Ashley. We have been friends for 28 years, we met in the first
grade. When were in elementary school, she would pass me notes
that said, "Are you still my friend? Circle yes or no". On my
stubborn days, I would circle "NO" and pass it back to her. She is
my sandbox friend. I exposed everything to Shawnise. She is the
friend that I did not calculate what I had already told her to see
what I could afford to tell her. She is very rational and has such a
soothing spirit. She thinks things through and then gives advice.
She moved to North Carolina for college and has been living there
since, so most of our venting sessions were long distance. She has
always made time for my crazy calls, it didn't matter if it was 4:00 in
the morning. She never suggested me to leave my family, but she
also thought that some of the things that I was telling her were flat
out ridiculous. She does have a breaking point though. I believe she
and I shared the same breaking point. One day I had came home
after working all day at the salon and I was tired. Earlier that day
Brandon had called me saying that the baby had ran out of milk. I
suggested that he go get some, and when I got home that night, I
realized that he never got the milk. I have always been that mother
that gets things done. If Brandon wasn't home and the kids needed
something I don't care if it was 11:00 at night, I would get them
dressed, put my daughter in the car and strap my son in the car seat
and be on my way. There were no excuses when it came to me
being a mother. For the life of me I couldn't comprehend the
reason why Brandon had not went out to get milk for the baby. He
was home all day with them, and waited for me to get home after

being on my feet all day to ask me to go to the store. He came to wake me up around 5 a.m. with the baby-crying, saying he needed some milk. I had to be up for work in less than an hour and I was exhausted. In the process of me getting ready he just started behaving very irate. I can't explain his actions. To me there is never a reason for a man to disrespect a woman and especially in front of her (let alone, THEIR) children. I was standing at the top of the stairs and he said, "You a anything a$$ b##ch". I said "wow, this is how you talk to me in front of your kids"? He said, "yeah f##k you b##ch, suck my d##k you anything a$$ b##ch". Our daughter at the time was 6 years old. I wanted to knock his head off his shoulders but I took the highroad. On my way to work I called his mother and told her what had just happened. She was very quiet and her response was, "so are you tired yet"? That is when I woke up and realized, "wow everyone else around me is tired from what is going on in my life, they are drained. If they are tired I sure as heck should be". That was the day that I became tired. I was tired of being disrespected with him coming home all hours of the night (sometimes not coming home at all), not answering his phone, leaving me with the kids all the time, not giving me the room for a mental break and the list goes on. I WAS TIRED!!! Us women usually leave mentally before physically leaving. I left MENTALLY when I was EXHAUSTED. He had drained all of my energy to the point that I had nothing left to give him. I needed God to give me a boost of energy for my kids and me. What good am I to them if I am not good for me? This was the breaking point for Shawnise and me. Everyone else had reached their breaking point a long time ago. It was just Shawnise and I battling these venting sessions, and this was the straw that broke the camel's back. Maybe the last straw should have been when he put me out of the car at 2 a.m. on the highway. I ended up walking on the wall that is off to the shoulder that starts out short, but gets higher as you drive by. I remember feeling scared to death. I was on the HIGHWAY on a weekend walking ALONE with a dead phone. That day I felt that he left me for dead, anything could have happened. I was walking up the wall thinking at some point it would come down, but it did not. Trust me this was NOT funny at the time, but now as I reflect on it, it's actually hilarious. Picturing anyone walking UP the wall on the HIGHWAY is beyond comical. The wall ended at its peak! This makes it even funnier. LOL. I eventually turned around and walked back down. I was crying and scared. Don't ask me how he ended up finding me that night. Remember my phone was dead? This night we were on our Ike and Tina ish. I remember getting back into the car and feeling like it was time for me to fight for my life. He had been drinking so he was acting a fool. I was scared in the car so I had to fake like I had to use the bathroom for him to let me out. He pulled over to a parking lot right by his mom's house and I got out. It was about 20 degrees outside. I squatted as if I was about to pee and TOOK OFF RUNNING! I looked back and he was running behind me. I remember he caught up with me and he jumped on my back. As I turned over he was standing over me, I wasn't sure what he was about to do, so I panicked and punched him dead in his eye. I had a white sweater on and blood started to drip on it. He was

10

panicking. "OMG! You are bleeding! I didn't hit you", he was drunk and confused. I played that to my advantage and told him that he did hit me. Brandon has never put his hands on me so he was really confused. We hopped in the car to drive to his mother's house. As we were driving he looked in the mirror and realized that it was him that was bleeding. He saw the gash that I had placed above his eye from using my left hand that carried the first rock that he put on my finger. He went off!! "Why would you hit me"? He screamed and yelled at me until we got to his mom's house. Once we got to his mother's and she opened the door, I was standing there with blood on my shirt, and he had blood on his coat and his face. She was like, "WHAT IN THE WORLD"?!! The rest of that night was a blur. I just remember her calling us "Ike and Tina" after that incident. Our relationship had become so emotionally drained at this point. It wasn't always like that, I can't even remember how or when it got to that point, but it began sometime after college. But, before I go deeper into our story, let me talk about them "College Days". This is where I had some of the best times of my life and also when I met Brandon. The first 2 years of college were all fun and games. I have a million stories to tell from college. Here is one that earned me, Tye, Ashley and Shanti (my other friend) our crew name "Ruff n Tuff". We all went to high school together, but I only knew them on a "hi and bye" basis. Tye and Ashley were best-friends in junior high school and they went to school with Shanti before high school, so they all had a history before I got to know them. On my first day on campus I saw them and immediately gravitated to them because they were familiar faces. We were all from DC surrounded by people from everywhere, so when I saw them it was like having a feeling of "home" on campus. We instantly formed a bond and hung out together when we weren't in class. We never started trouble, but trouble seemed to find us. Freshman year tested our "gangsta" real quick. One day we were at a flag football game when an argument between my girlfriend Ashley and another girl started. It started over the girl saying something about her not liking Ashley's eyebrows. I know, stupid right? Anyway, they were going back and forth and I could slowly see the argument escalating. When I walked by the girl and her friends, I heard the girl say, "I am going to beat her a$$", referring to Ashley. I immediately reported the message to Ashley. "Ohh she said she going to beat somebody a$$", I was laughing when I said it but in the "I-wishabishwould" tone. Ashley didn't take that threat lightly, everyone was trying to calm her down. I assumed that they had everything under control so I stepped off. When I came back they were all in the gym, the argument got louder, people were holding each other back and I thought I saw a fight going on. My eyes zoomed in on the girl that was running her mouth about Ashley and I transformed into crazy "Ki". I kicked my shoes off and started to march towards the girl. WHOP! I punched that girl so hard in her face it sounded like I smacked her. After that, all I remember is one of the guys snatching me off of her and me still trying to get back at her. I think one of my breasts popped out my shirt and everything. It required someone big and strong enough to be able to get me off of the girl. Whoever grabbed me literally threw me on his shoulder and carried me out the building. Immediately after I was reported to the campus police. After talking with them and the school, I had to wait on them to make a final decision. They wanted to put me off of campus immediately, but the river of tears I cried might have contributed to them having a little mercy on me. They sent me back to my room that night and said they would let me know in the days to follow if I could stay at the school or not. That immediately stressed me out because I knew that my grandparents would have killed me if I got put out. After the fight and the meeting, I was walking down the hill and a girl said, "yeah I heard the girl in the red shirt got her a$$ beat"! I envisioned myself attacking her, but the only thing that stopped me was when I looked down and saw I had on a pink shirt. The girl I fought was the girl in the red shirt. The next day I woke up and my body was hurting!! It felt like I had worked out after not working out in a while, my entire body was sore. If you have never been in a fight I will be happy to describe it to you. It is not like how it is when you are fighting your siblings or cousins, with those fights you feel very much present and you can feel each blow. In a real fight, after the first blow, it feels like you are dreaming, I have never felt anything in a real fight until after. I ended up getting 2 years of academic probation and that was them being very gracious. The girl's mother was trying to press charges, but never did, THANK GOD. I did not see that girl again on campus until a few days later. We were in the cafe and I happened to walk past her. When we connected eyes, I realized how hard I had it her. Her whole eye was black and swollen. This fight and how hard we went for each other is when the guys on campus named us "Ruff n Tuff". We were the girls on campus that the guys liked to hang around. We were fun, funny, down to earth and all around cool. We were not prissy and stuck up. We didn't have to get "cute" around guys. We didn't go to class in heels, lipstick and a beat down face. We went in hoodies, sweats, no make-up, jeans, and tees on most days. We had a very 90-ish style about us. This was before all the butt shots, weaves, frontals, and eyebrows on "fleek" days. Don't get me wrong, we knew how to do it when It was time to be done. We got real dolled up on our club nights. Those nights were so much fun. We would blast our go-go, do our makeup, do each other's hair, put together our outfits, and just have a pre-game party right in our rooms. When it was time to go, we would go downstairs to the "circle" and hop on the club bus, which was a cheese bus. No shame! LOL. This was before uber and lift. In Baltimore they had "hacks", basically this was hitch hiking, and that wasn't too safe. The circle was where you got picked up and dropped off. If you had a circle window view, you had front row seats to all the action. You found out a lot from the "circle". Who was dealing with who, who drove what car, what time someone got in, what time they left, the circle was the Wendy Williams "hot tea" spot. I even found out this guy that I was talking to was dealing with another girl on campus from looking out the window down on to the circle. I saw his car pull up and I was looking for my phone about to call him thinking he was there for me, until I saw a girl get out the car. Oh yeah, fights!! Fights went down in the circle too! Oh, and drunk episodes. The circle was the stage for a lot of our entertainment. College life was lit. We would have some of the best on campus dorm parties. This was before Facebook and instagram so the experiences were never on the "gram", and today I thank God for that. We lived in the moment. Phones weren't a real distraction. Back then, we had flip phones. In fact I still had a phone that I had to press one number 3 times to type one letter. We talked more on the phone back then. We ate oodles and noodles on the regular. There was no uber eats. Everything was not at our disposal. We did not live our lives by comparing our lives to someone on social media, which was non-existent. There was no social media beefs, videos going viral, or even group chats. Our group chats were in person. We would all get together in our rooms (or wherever else) and have live group chats. The only screen shots we had were our memory. There were no iPhone pictures. We took pictures with our cameras and took them to CVS to get them developed! Our phones were not our eyes. Right now, many of us do not get to experience real life because of our phones. Sometimes you miss the moment that you are in because you are viewing it through your phone. I saw a video of Beyoncé and she was singing to one of her fans while they were recording her on their phone. She stopped the music, and said something along the lines of, "I am IN YOUR FACE. You aren't able to take in the moment because you have your phone out". I can't remember exactly what it was but that was the just of it. Just think about it. Now days, everywhere we go we have our phones with us. Our phones are our pacifiers. We throw tantrums when we don't have them. We sometimes can't even think without them. In college we did not even have GPS. If I wanted to get somewhere I would have to go to the library and print the directions off of map quest. Even that, to some people reading this is a luxury, if you grew up in an era where you had to use an actual map. We did not grow up in this (now what they call) "microwave" era. Nothing came to us easy, if we wanted something we had to go out and get it. If we wanted a job, we had to apply in-person in most cases. If I lived my college years in the times that we are in now I do not think that I would have had the same experiences, in fact, I know that I wouldn't. My phone would have stolen all of my memories and experiences. God forbid I were to loose my phone, I wouldn't have access to those memories. I would have depended on the phone to remember everything for me. My memory isn't as good now as it was then, I think it is because I use my phone to capture so much that I am not as present as I should be in the moment. My memories from some of the best times in my college days are branded in my brain. A phone wasn't able to rob me of that. I challenge you to put the phone down sometimes and just enjoy life. Savor the moment. Life is short, it's even shorter with your phone in your hand 24/7. Imagine how much you could do if you just PUT YOUR PHONE DOWN. I am able to write a book because I chose to put my phone down. Let that sink in. I am able to WRITE A BOOK! I am typing, I am writing, I am not using the microwave version of telling someone my experiences and having them do the work for me. Don't be that person that scrolled your life away. Don't be so busy watching the life of others that yours just pass you by. Now that you have got some stories from my college life with my girls, let me get back to Brandon. When

PRESS ON

Brandon and I first got together at 19 it was pure bliss. You know how you meet a guy and don't initially like him and end up liking him later? That is how our relationship began. We were in our freshman year in college when we met. I went to Coppin State and he went to Morgan State in Baltimore, MD. One day we had a go-go at my school and I met him at the "let out". I don't remember paying him too much attention but apparently he was paying me the most attention. He is obsessed with my feet so that is one of the first things that really had him going, I had my open toe shoes on that day. He saw my feet before he saw me. My friends and his friends were all standing in front of the dorms conversing. His words to me that night were, "You think I'm sexy"? I looked at him with the "ugh face" because I absolutely hate arrogance and said, "I mean, you ight". Yeah I thought he was attractive, but I wasn't attracted to him with that weak line. That night we exchanged numbers, and I did not wait on him to call me. I had a boyfriend at the time and I guess I was being loyal to him. Eventually, Brandon called and we would talk from time to time on the phone. But, I still didn't like him. I was just entertaining him with convo when I felt like it. He would ask me out all the time and each time I had a different excuse as to why I couldn't go. He was just too pressed and that was a turn off for me. I was the type that more so liked a challenge. I didn't really pay too much attention to guys when they were too pressuring. Brandon was one of the guys I was entertaining in my down time. I would be on the phone with him and my cousin would call and I would be like; "girl, this clown is on the other line. I am going to put you on 3-way. Don't SAY

NOTHING". When he would get off of the phone we would BURST into laughter!! I didn't take anyone serious, it was my first year in college. Yeah I had a little boyfriend, but the fun I was having with my friends made me care much less about a boyfriend. There were so many guys at school alone that wanted my attention, but never got it. I would come to my room from class to secret letters and notes under my door. I would always hear about someone liking me, but I did not care the least bit. There wasn't anyone that sparked my interest that much. I would talk and I do mean just that TALK to about 5 guys at a time, none of which I ever took serious. I was just living the "college life"; going to class, having minor crushes, and blowing refund checks. Tye always liked Brandon for me. She would be like, "I really like Brandon". In my head I would be like "that's cool, I don't". I still didn't make time to go on a date with him. Many times I would ignore his calls, or when I would answer I would say, "Let me call your "right" RIGHT back". Chile I would call a week later, if not longer than that. This went on for about a year. One day I said, "Let me call Brandon". I called him and he had the nerve to tell me that he would call ME "right" RIGHT back. He gave me a huge dose of my own medicine. As much as he called me, and as much as I told him the same thing, I did not like that he was pulling a me on ME. I thought about him that whole night and for the first time I had to train myself on not to call him. I remember calling him back a few days later because he NEVER CALLED me back. Our lines had reversed. I called and said, "Thanks for calling me back". His response was, "my bad I was busy". I was completely stuck, yet intrigued. This was now a challenge for me and I was up for it. I went back to my room that night (Tye and I were roommates at the time) and talked to Tye. We were having our regular girl session and I was laying on my twin bed with my feet on the wall and I said to her, "I think I like Brandon". She was like, "For real? Aww. I like Brandon". Then it hit me, I sat up like "NO, Tye! I LIKE BRANDON"! I was shocked by the words that came out of my mouth. Then the words became a question. "I like Brandon"? (neck leaning to the side) "OMG, I like Brandon". It went from a question to a fact real quick. Now I had to figure out how to get him back under my wing. I don't remember how I did it, but I did. Oh yeah, that boyfriend I had, I broke up with him. He was doing his own thing anyway. That call was simple. He answered and I said, "I can't go with you no more". He was like, "Dag. For real. Ok." and that was the end of that. I finessed my way back to the ball being in my court with Brandon, and we went on our first date to The Cheesecake Factory at the Baltimore Harbor. I remember being so nervous that I did not even eat my food and I was starving. I was afraid of eating in front of guys that I liked, so I didn't eat on our first date. The date went really good and this was the start to our puppy love relationship. Soon become inseparable. He would pick me up from school in his Jeep on a regular basis. The infamous Jeep had a spoon on the side where the adjuster was for the seat. When I would get in, he would reach over and bend the spoon to angle the seat where it was comfortable for me. The heat only worked when his foot was on the gas. I would be freezing at every stoplight. We literally started from the bottom together.

Brandon is by far one of the sweetest and caring guys I have ever met. He would open the doors for me, take me on random dates, come to my dorm baring gifts, he was just the bomb. I love surprises and he was the king of them. I would come down to check him at the front desk to my dorm and he would be standing there with flowers on random days. The sweet gestures and surprises continued throughout our 11-year relationship. He is the type that does things that the average man is not thinking about. We were at the club once and there was a man in the club selling bouquets of roses. Brandon called him over and asked how much they were, I think they were maybe $10, I can't remember. He said, "Give me all of them"! The man was shocked and so was I! I can not remember how many bouquets there were but they were a lot. There were enough for the man to give me the entire bucket. Brandon set the tone of being romantic so high! He would always say, "yeah if a ni##a comes after me he is going to have a rough time showing you what I already have". He has been everything that I have wished for in a guy when it came to his thoughtfulness. One time we went on a date and when I came out of the restaurant, I saw a horse and carriage waiting with the guy that greets you to say "Madam" while he reaches for your hand. I said, "look Brandon! Isn't that nice"? He looked and said, "dag that is nice. That's for you. Come on"! That night on the horse and carriage, I felt like a Princess. This is a sample of what Brandon would do on a regular Tuesday night, no special occasion, these were "just because" gestures. When I turned 25, Brandon threw me the best surprise birthday. I remember hinting around that I would

love to have a surprise birthday party, but I did not expect one.
The weekend after my birthday, we are going to a club on a regular
night and when we got there the man at the door said, "ya'll here
for the birthday girl"? I said, "no". I was confused, but did not pay
too much attention to it. As I walked up the stairs, they stamped
my hand, and as soon as my foot hit the floor all I heard was
"SURPRISE"!!! I burst into tears. I was truly surprised. Every time
I turned to look at someone I would cry because I was so
overwhelmed. All of my high-school friends were there, my
childhood friends, my family, and so many important people in my
life. I was so touched that all of them had taken the time out to
show me that much love. The décor was amazing. Everything
about it said "Rickia". My name was up on the bar. My favorite
candy (m&m's) was in bowls on the bar. I said "Omg Brandon you
know I love m&m's", he said, "I know, look at them". When I
looked at them, they became much more special. They said "Happy
Birthday Rickia" and "Love Brandon". The bar was open and
Jamaican food was catered. He even got me an ice sculpture! It
read "Happy 25th Birthday Rickia". This day was one of the best
days in my life. On our 9-year anniversary he took me to the Chart
House on the water. When we got there they greeted me with a
dozen of roses, from Brandon, of course. He is so charming and
just when I think he can't surprise me anymore, he always outdoes
himself. I ordered my drink and in came another dozen of roses!
"OMG! Thank you", I said to the waiter and Brandon. He gets so
much joy out of my face lighting up like a parent sitting watching
their kids open their Christmas gifts. I looked at the menu and it

read "Happy 9 year Anniversary Rickia and Brandon". Another antic of Brandon thinking out every detail. The waiter came AGAIN with another dozen roses, I was like "What in the world"!!!? Just when I thought I could not get any happier or surprised. After the 3rd dozen, more came. Every 20 minutes they came out with another dozen. We were one of the only black couples in the restaurant. Many people looked over and said "congrats", others looked and whispered. I left that restaurant with NINE dozen roses that represented the 9 years that we had been together. I could go on for years about the most thoughtful, loving surprises from Brandon. I truly adore his charming ways.

When we were 19 he said that he was going to marry me and I believed him. At that age everything seems believable. Brandon had become a familiar face on my school campus because he was there all the time. We practically lived together in my junior year. I stayed with him on the days that he didn't stay with me and vice versa. We enjoyed each others company so much and at a young age I could see a big future with him. He became my best friend, he knew everything about me, and certain things I have only shared with him, until now. I had my first health scare in college and only shared it with Brandon. But, I want to publically share it now because it may help someone else. I went for my first pap smear in college. I did not know what to expect because I had never had one before. The only expectation that I had was that everything would be normal. The days that followed my appointment were care free, I wasn't worried about anything. That is until the doctor called me and said that I needed to come in to get my results, because they were not normal. That call scared me to death. I went into a panic, I tried my best to calm myself down but I could not. I was thinking every bad situation that I could imagine. When I went to get the results from my doctor, I did even understand what she was saying. She was very mean, and that did not make me feel at ease. She said, "you have a mild case of HPV". All I heard was the "H" and the "V", and I mentally passed out at that point. I had never heard of HPV and she barely explained to me what it was. I could only understand certain words and one of those words were "pre-cancerous", and all I heard from that was the cancerous part. I sat in her office and cried my heart out and she was not at all comforting. She just laid it on thick with no regards to my feelings and left me in the room crying. When I left, I called Brandon and I was screaming at the top of my lungs crying. I thought that this was the end. He could not understand either, because I couldn't explain something that I did not understand. For those that do not know, HPV is sexually transmitted by skin-to-skin and condoms do not fully protect you against it. Most cases of cervical cancer are associated with HPV. Now that they have a preventative vaccine for it (something that they did not have at the time I found out), it was no doubt in my mind that I would make sure that I got it for my kids to protect them. I don't ever want them to feel like how I felt that day. About 80% of sexually active people are infected with HPV at some point of their lives. Now, I am no loose goose, never have been, but Brandon was not my first and this was my first time getting a pap so it just as well could have been from a previous relationship. I am not that girl that many guys can say they have had. DC is very small and many people know a lot of the same people. If someone says that they slept with me there is a 99.9% chance that they are lying. I take my single digit count with pride. But, all it takes is one time, with one person, to create a situation that will change your life forever. After that bad news, Brandon and I did our own research. He printed information on it and gave it to me and we educated each other. We put those papers inside my pillow and every chance we got, we got on our knees and prayed over it. I never told my friends because I was actually embarrassed. After my biopsy, I was due for a pap every 3-4 months to monitor it. We continued to pray over it. A year later, I got a letter in the mail that said that all of my results were NORMAL!! I know we are currently living in a time where being sexually free is praised. I am not shaming anyone's "body count" because all it takes is ONE body to count your life out. But, in a world of Thotiana's bussing it down, I would like to give some advice that I would give my daughter or to a young girl that may be reading this. My advice is to be very selective. Make smart decisions for yourself and your future. You want to be the girl that a guy thinks about potentially hurting and decides for YOUR best interest, it is best not to deal with you. You are worthy of a guy getting back to you once he is fully ready to commit. We all have a past and can never change it. However, we have a future lined up too. It is never too late to make changes. Once they are done with these Thotiana's, they are going to go looking for the Smartiana's to marry and settle down with. Hold yourself at a higher standard.

PRESS ON

Position yourself for a man to have to step up to be in your presence. Further more position yourself to be perfectly ok with no one being in your presence. Be secure with who you are and know what your hand calls for. Sometimes riding the wave will wash you out this world. It was Gods grace and mercy that has saved me from many situations. Every pap result from then on has been normal!! God's grace is when he gives you what you deserve. God's mercy is when he gives you in spite of. This was a huge example of God's mercy. He gave me mercy, in spite of me living in the sin of fornication.

Around our 4th year in college we started to get more into ourselves and doing our own things. I was permanently living with Brandon and we were playing house and going to school. My friends and I were still linking up but not how we were those first few years when we were all living on campus. Brandon and I still had a very loving and fun filled relationship. We were becoming adults. We both worked government jobs when we did not have class. We were paying bills and entering the real world. With us being together at such a young age most of our first time events were with each other. Brandon taught me how to "drive" drive. He went with me to get my first car that I actually drove, (I had one before but never drove it) a 96" green caddy that my grandfather got me. I got my first apartment with him. Many of my most memorable moments were with Brandon. We have celebrated life together for so long that I couldn't really imagine celebrating anything without him. At the young age of 23 we had our first child together. I always tell people, you get to know a person when you live together but you really get to know them when you have kids together. Looking back on my life 23 is a very young age to have children. If I may encourage someone reading this for a second, I would like to tell you if you are young and want to have children, that is great, children are a blessing. But, live life first. Travel the world, save some money, buy a house, get married, there are so many things that you can experience before doing so. Having children should not be you trying to punch the clock. Live a lot before having children and live a lot after having children. Don't feel pressured. We had our daughter at an age not just numerical, but time wise where we just weren't ready. I was pregnant my last year of college. I had no career lined up and no plan. I was working at the IRS, which may have potentially been a permanent opportunity for me, but it wasn't. I was in a stay-in-school program and my manager discussed potential opportunities for me once I completed school. Her thoughts on that changed when I told her that I was 5 months pregnant. I was hiding my pregnancy from my job. I remember going into her office and informing her that I was with child and her response was, "so are you going to keep it"? I looked at her like "if I didn't have plans on keeping my baby I wouldn't be sitting here telling you that I was pregnant". This lady tried to convince me that I was making the wrong decision by keeping MY baby, which was not her place. I continued to work that job until I walked across the stage 9 months pregnant with a 3.98 GPA! I was so proud of myself. I pushed through despite what people thought and believed. I remember calling my grandmother on many days and nights crying and expressing to her that I wasn't sure how I would finish, and how stressful school was for me. I was taking 21 credits my last semester. I had "morning" sickness ALL DAY. On the days that I did not have class I literally slept all day. I would somehow wake up at sometimes 3 a.m. and study for a test that I had at 8 a.m. and actually PASS. This was one of the most trying times of my LIFE. Going through my pregnancy with my daughter let me know that I can do any and everything that I put my mind to. I amazed myself graduating college and being one of the top students of my class. Throughout my time in college I saw so many girls get pregnant, take a "break", and never come back. My mind was set up, I was not taking a break. A break for me was too close to comfort for me to becoming a "drop out". I finished strong.

When I graduated from college, Brandon and I both moved home to his mother's house to prepare for our first-born child. We were raised differently. His mom raised him and my grandparents raised me. How we were raised played a major role in our parenting.

2 MOLDING
THIS IS WHAT SHAPED ME

I was raised by my grandparents and I thank God for them taking a major role in my life. They showed me what structure is. They created a home for my sister and I. My mother had us young and did not really know how to be a mother to us at that time. For as long as I can remember, I grew up in my grandparent's house 90% of the time. I have always known order in their house and I experienced a lot of love in their home. "I love you" was said all day everyday. My grandmother was the backbone of the house. She made sure we went to the best private schools, enrolled us in the best dance schools and camps, she even made us take a class on etiquette. I learned a lot about being a woman from her. I find myself acting a lot like her as an adult. She would spend hours decorating our Christmas tree and that is no exaggeration, now when Christmas comes I am doing the same thing. I did not start crossing my legs at the thigh until I was an adult. "Little girls cross their legs at their ankles", she would say. I teach my daughter the same thing. "You don't say "fart", that is unlady like, "you say pass gas". We were taught to always carry ourselves with class. Every Sunday she had us in church. She dressed us alike probably until we were the ages of 9 and 10. On Sundays, we wore the best of dresses and coats. We had fur coats, white dresses, slips, tights, nice dress shoes, you name it. She even polished our shoes when they would get the least bit of scratches on them. For Easter, she would start getting us ready way ahead of time. Everything had to be perfect. At night she rolled our front bang with pink sponge rollers and tied it down. Sunday morning, our hair was laid, our dresses were fluffed, our stockings were white, our shoes were polished, our earrings were on, our faces were greased, and our purses were strapped over our shoulders. She dressed us just like the grandchildren of the Queen of England. I have pictures to prove it. My grandmother is one of those people that don't intend to be funny but she is. Many times some of her actions aren't funny until years later. When we were teenagers, my sister, me, and my best friend Lawanda wanted to go to a go-go (D.C. party). We begged her to go and surprisingly she said that we could. She dropped us off and had a long speech with the three of us stating that if we were not outside at the time she said she was picking us up, she was going to come on the stage and embarrass us. I never doubted for a second that she would do that because she was the queen of embarrassing us. Not only did she drop us off, but she got out the car to check the scene. Sniffing around outside she said, "smells like reefer"! Even today she never says weed, she says reefer. LOL.

We just knew after that observation, she was going to change her mind, but surprisingly she did not. She let us live that night. I can go on and on about stories with her. 9/11 is a day that many of us remember vividly. It was one of the scariest days of my life! We were in high school and we watched the twin towers go down on live television. Everyone was scared and crying. Before I knew it, everyone was getting called to the front desk for early dismissal. I was impatiently waiting on them to call my sister and I. That was the longest wait of my life. When we got downstairs, my grandmother was there waiting in her pajamas, rollers, and bonnet. She looked at us with tears in her eyes and said, "THE UNITED STATES IS BEING BOMBED"!! Can you imagine how scary that would be hearing that as an adult, let alone a child!? Later, my grandfather said, "ahh man, now why would she tell ya'll that"!? She would serve us news very raw! No cut cards. Sometimes I can't handle her approach because it's too blunt for me. We spent that whole day and even the weeks to follow scared for our lives. Every time we heard a plane we thought it was coming towards where we were. I think I still have PTSD from 9/11. After that happened, there would be these really loud jets flying over our high school, and they were so loud that there was no doubt in my head that they were coming into the building. I would jump up and run for the door in the middle of class because the noise triggered my anxiety. Because of the struggles that I have had with anxiety, I have kept bad news away from my grandmother just to keep myself a little calmer. She is always calm in situations that would scare me. She was like super woman. There were many times that I watched her literally protect us. One night, we were coming home and we were walking to our house and there was a man walking towards us with a gun, I panicked. I did not know what that man might have done. Gramma stayed calm and just kept walking. The truest, yet scariest line that she says is, "if it's your time to go, ain't nothing you can do about it. Ain't no sense in freakin' out". She doesn't fear death. That may be why she is so raw with her delivery. She says things that she can handle, but I may not necessarily be able to. One time we were on 16th street in northwest D.C. and in the middle of traffic we got caught in a drug bust. All I remember is all these guys running with guns, the police was chasing them with guns, and everyone outside was panicking. It was just like something out of a movie. She prepared us for whatever was coming, even if it was death. She made us duck on the floor in the back seat and pressed our bodies down. There was no way that she could duck, because she needed to see a visible way for us to get out of harm's way. She started to pray over all of us for our protection. We lived to tell that story, and just like Super Woman, she saved another day. My grandmother was like a Clair Huxtable as I was growing up. She has been nothing short of classy. She was one of the top advertisers at her job, she drove fly cars, she wore minks, furs, nice dress suits, her hair and nails were always done, she was the epitome of what a woman of class should be. She still is. Education was top priority in our house. In the summer time when everyone was out running and playing, my sister and I were on the porch stuck until we finished our 3 page book reports that she assigned us. We used to hate that! She made us read 2-3 books a week during the summer.

On Saturday's she would wake us up at the crack of dawn to help her pull grass, plant flowers and water plants. Omg, we hated that with a passion. Especially me, I had the worst allergies and being out there in those plants would have my eyes watering, nose running, and me constantly sneezing. So many of these things that we hated, I now appreciate. I learned what an independent woman looked like. When she wanted something, she went out and got it. I remember her going to buy her ruby red Mercedes, it went perfect with her signature red lipstick. My grandmother would hug and kiss on us all the time. She read us bedtime stories at night, taught us our night prayers and molded us so much. I thank God for her everyday. My sister would say that she is "grammas" favorite and "everyone knows it", and to some extent I have believed that. I don't think that Rence' was loved any more than me, but I think that she was more attended to. I find myself thinking that my grandmother was trying to overcompensate on love with Rence' because her father was not around. Rence' was the baby, and she was definitely "gramma's baby". I often felt like Rence' could do no wrong in her eyes. One time we were getting into trouble because Rence' had done something and she kept blaming me for it. I kept saying, "SHE IS LYING" and she really was but no, her "Rence' Berg" was "right". She said "Rickia, all you do is lie, and you are still lying", that hurt me because she didn't give me the benefit of the doubt. I didn't bother snitching too much from that point on because it wasn't like she was going to believe me over Rence' anyway. I noticed the difference more when I got older. Sometimes, I would sneak and call my father and tell him about something that she did or said I did not like. He would pop up to the house and that would create more issues. They would get into big arguments and he would say, "my daughter can live with ME, she doesn't HAVE to be here"! I would sit on the steps and watch them argue and curse each other out and feel so torn. My grandfather would step in to diffuse it. Some of those arguments got really bad. Later, I would hear her in her room crying. When I would come in she would tell me that she does everything to take care of us and I only call my father when it was an issue with her that I did not like. I would feel so bad.

My grandmother is not my mother's biological mother. I did not find that out until I was about 8 and I was so upset that my mother told me. I wish that she never told me. My grandmother raised my mother since she was a baby, so she is the only grandmother I have really ever known. She is a phenomenal woman to take on someone else's child AND their children and raise them as her own. My grandmother and I clashed often as I was growing up. I think that I reminded her of my mother more than Rence' did, and that may have been why she was a little closer to her. My mother and grandmother have always had a love-hate relationship, something I can't describe because I wasn't there when my mother was growing up. But, I have seen some pretty nasty arguments between the two. My mother has no filter, she may be able to cut a person with her words. When they would get into arguments she would slice my grandmother up with words and I would sit on the stairs in complete shock. I mean they would be up in each other's faces like they were about to fight! My grandfather would be there to diffuse those situations as well.

The underlined "favoritism" with Rence' became more vivid in my eyes as we got older. When it was time for prom she took me to Macys so that I may find a dress, and it was not to be expensive. Cool, I was a size 0, I found something fast, that wasn't hard. The night of prom she made it very clear that she would be outside at 2:30 a.m., and if I was not outside she was coming in to get me. I was waiting at the door on time to save myself the embarrassment. I missed the whole prom after party. Even my date stayed and he didn't even go to my school. A year later when it was time for "Rence' Berg" to go to prom, oh we were getting prepared like she was getting married. Beloved was getting custom made dresses and such! You know who sat up and waited for "miss thang" to get home? ME! I was watching the clock while my grandmother SLEPT like a newborn baby. No one was waiting for Rence' outside at 2:30 am. I fell asleep watching the clock, when I woke up the sun was up and she was just coming in the door. This for me was the ultimate act of favoritism. Honestly, I would rather Rence' be gramma's favorite versus me because she is more sensitive than I am. I can handle not being in the "favorite" seat.

I've always felt me accomplishing my goals in life were very questionable to my grandmother. I felt like she doubted me a lot. One day we were in the grocery store and I am not sure what transpired her to say this, but she said; "You are going to be just like your mother. You will probably barely graduate high school and IF you do go to college you will probably only go to UDC". It hurts for me to put that in this book because I don't want to hurt her by revisiting what she said that hurt me. She may not ever remember saying that. Those were some of the stickiest words in my life. No matter how much I tried to put them in the back of my head they still whispered in my ear through my life. These words made me push myself past my limits. I spent my entire 5 years of college using those words to push me. I wanted to make her proud and prove her wrong at the same time. Me graduating from college made me feel like I killed those two birds in one stone. My grandmother still plays an essential role in my life. Although what she said to me really hurt, it helped me prepare for real life. I now do the unexpected. Writing this book was very unexpected! I always push myself to do the things that people believe I can't do. I turned that very negative comment into something very positive. The cup in my eyes is always half full. I thank God for my grandmother over and over again. I needed her in my life. I would not be nowhere near where I have gotten if it were not for her. She is one of my biggest cheerleaders. She always tells me how proud of me that she is. She is always encouraging me, and pushing me to do better. She speaks all positivity over my life. I've always looked at her and admired the woman that she has been. She has set the tone of what qualities I wanted to posses in being a woman. I am the woman that I am today because I had a grandmother that took on the role of being exactly that, a GRAND-mother. I got to see her be everything grand; a grandmother, a grand-wife, a grand-woman, and now a grand-great-grand-mother. She is my grand, a hunnid grand. Pause. Message to my gramma: I never would have made it without you gramma, I love you and thank you for all you have done for me and continue to do.

While we are on the grand-train, let me introduce ya'll to my grandfather. This man is the coolest man that I have ever seen walk this earth. He is so smoove. If he ever yells, he is really pissed off! When he comes into a room he just glides right on in. Aside from all the Bill Cosby drama, my grandfather was Cliff Huxtable. Now that I think about it, my grandparent's house was like growing up on the Cosby's. I could completely relate to that show growing up. He even dressed like Cliff, no, maybe a little more fly. He definitely keeps those Huxtable sweaters on deck. Rence' would say that I am "deddy's favorite", I would deny that accusation. We do have a very special relationship though. Anything that I have ever needed for my grandfather to do, he has always done. He taught me how to ride my bike. He even taught me how to jump rope. He was big on health and exercise. His favorite health question is, "Did you drink water"? "War-Ter"? Anything that was wrong, water was brought up.

Me: "Deddy, I am sleepy."

Him: "War-Ter"

Me: "Deddy, it's hot!"

PRESS ON

Him: "When was the last time you drank some war-ter?"

That is no typo, there was big emphasize on "WAR-TER". In the mornings he would make my sister and I drink a teaspoon of cod-liver oil, this was the absolute worst thing ever to taste for me. My grandfather made me figure things out on my own. I would ask him how to spell something and he would never tell me, he would say, "look in the dictionary". That never made sense to me. How in the world am I going to look up something that I can not spell? This was not in the day where Google was around and I could type it in wrong, and it will say "did you mean" whatever they think you meant. All we had was a hand held dictionary and I would be completely lost looking for a word that required me to READ that whole letter section. To find "demise" I would have to read every "d" word until I found it. I wouldn't know if it was "d-a", "d-u", "d-e", "d-i", or what ever other letter combinations it sounds like. This slowed up my homework so much. He would let me look through it on my own for an hour and finally show me where it was in the dictionary. LOL.

Growing up, my grandfather was very Black Power-ish. He taught us how powerful we are at a young age. He may not have made us write book reports or pull grass on Saturday mornings, but he would sure enough pop in Roots and have us sit for 2 weeks watching it waiting for it to end. Watching that movie gave me an instant headache. When the movie Amistad came out, I'm sure he pre-ordered our tickets. Our most celebrated holiday for him was the Million Man March. He also marched on Washington with Martin Luther King. He was serious about black marches. For events like this, it was ok to miss school. Get out the books and into this BLACK skin! I don't think my grandfather could live an any blacker life. I may have been a baby black panther and not have even known. One day I told him that I wished on a troll doll (a toy that you made a wish on) that I were white, with blonde hair, and blue eyes. He lectured me on hours about how we were the first people, and I should be proud and embrace my beautiful blackness. Even now as an adult, he does not like me to wear blonde hair. For him to finally be ok with it, I had to Google images of kids darker than him in Africa with blonde hair and even some with light eyes. I proved my point that day, WE come in all colors and shades, even our hair! My grandfather is very rooted. He knows his history, and he made sure to let us know it as well.

On my grandfather's off days, he would always cook breakfast. His off days were some of my best mornings. The smell of his fried potatoes, waffles and bacon would be my alarm clock when he was off. My grandfather gave me the best examples of what a man should look be. I have never heard him call my grandmother out her name, I have never seen him disrespect her. Over all, he is to me how a man should carry himself. A man should carry himself as a man, period, no matter how much a woman pushes him.

When I was little, I would put my ear to his back and just listen to him talk with my eyes closed. I would inhale the moment that I was

38

enjoying with his spirit, then exhale the thought of me growing up and not being able to do those things. My grandfather and I have always shared a special relationship. I would definitely say that I am a "deddy's" girl. I can not think of anything that my grandfather has said or done to me that caused me pain. He has been one of my biggest cheerleaders. He has supported everything that I have done. I take that back, there was one time that I was hurt by my grandfather's actions. When I had to face him and tell him that I was pregnant with my daughter, that was the moment that I felt I let him down for the first time in life. When I told him, he sat very quietly, and I literally watched one tear fall from his eye. That one tear pierced my soul. If I had ever let anyone down in life, it was to the ones that let me down. But, letting down someone that has never let me down hurt me. He wiped that one tear, gave me a hug, a kiss and said it was going to be ok. When it was time to tell my mothers side of the family that I was pregnant, I was scared and embarrassed to even utter the words, "I am pregnant". My grandfather told me that I needed to tell the family at Thanksgiving Dinner. I was so nervous the entire time. Now my mother, she would have showed up with an "I'm Pregnant" t- shirt and said eff whoever thought whatever. But this was me, I cared too much about what they would say or think. They suspected something was up the way I skipped over my aunts Shrimp gumbo. They usually blame me and my other aunt for eating all the shrimp. That particular year I wasn't even in the equation for them to blame me. My grandfather nudged my arm for me to tell one of my aunts when I was in the kitchen, and I just could not. He then said,

"Rickia has some good news, go ahead and tell them". My anxiety came attempting to kick me in my back to the floor. I instantly started to cry and he rubbed my back and said, "she is having a baby". His entire approach to the family let them know that he had my back, this was a good thing, and he was not going to allow any room for me to be shunned in his presence. Just like he has supported me in everything that I have done before, he showed his support in my pregnancy. I secretly promised myself that I would make sure that I still made him proud, baby and all. Having my grandfather in my life was essential. I thank God for him.

My grandparents filled the void of my parents, but they could never replace them. They stayed married for over 30 years, and divorced my 2nd or 3rd year in college. The divorce completely took me by surprise. Growing up in my grandparent's house I did not see too much arguing or fighting. Whatever was going on in their marriage went on behind closed doors so I did not have many details on their marital issues. Them getting divorced was heartbreaking to me because the home that I once knew was no longer there. They sold the house. When I was younger, I remember getting mad and saying to myself, "I can't wait to get out of this house". I should have been more careful with my words. In that house I learned what a family should look like. We sat at the table and ate dinner together. I learned my grace in that house. I learned a woman's role as a wife in that house. I learned how a man should take care of his family in that house and so much more. I am thankful that the divorce did not happen until my sister and I were adults. Although we were both affected by it, I think we were able to take it in better because we were adults. I remember when we were packing everything to move and I was looking around thinking "this is really it". Sometimes I wish I could go back just to inhale the memories of that house. I wish I could walk down to the basement and breathe in the fear I had as a little girl running up the stairs thinking there was a ghost behind me. I wish I could rub my hands on the yellow rigid walls, and remember how I would brush my hands on them while walking down the stairs, and see my grandfather there sleep with his hat over his eyes. I wish that I could go upstairs and click the hard light switch in the bathroom and stare and the pink tile on the wall. I remember how I would sit in that tub and play Joe "I wanna know", while thinking about my little boyfriend that broke my heart in the 9th grade. I wish that I could walk the hall that lead to my grandparent's room, and look to the right to see my grandmother sit for an hour and do her skin care regimen, while she watched the news. Wishful thinking. Even if I could go back just to inhale the feelings, the memories, and the experiences I had in each room, I couldn't. The whole house is different. The rooms that once were are no longer there. The entire house has been remodeled so I would get lost trying to backtrack what once was. I'm sure with the new paint, walls being torn down, new rooms built, and whatever other changes, I couldn't inhale the smell of that house if I sniffed the floors searching for it. Home has a smell. As much as I said to myself as a kid "I can't WAIT to get out of this house", I truly regretted that when reality sank in. My grandparents getting divorced ended in me no longer having "home" to go home to.

Brandon's mother's house was the home I wished for when I was younger. Growing up in DC, I wished to live in a nice house in Maryland and her house was the Maryland house I wished to live in. I had this wish way before gentrification swarmed the city. This was when the city was something we wanted to get away from. She moved to Maryland from D.C. when Brandon was in high school. She made me feel right at home as she helped us prepare for this new angel that we were expecting. Our daughter's due date was May 31st and his mother's birthday is June 5th. We would joke all the time and I would say, "what if this baby came on your birthday"? She would call her friends and say, "guess what I am getting for my birthday"? And when they would say "What"? She would say "a granddaughter". As we prepared to have the baby I got a little depressed. All of my friends were out living life and I was not able to participate in some of the fun because I was pregnant. I was excited about having the baby but it seems like she took forever to come. One day I went for my checkup and they said that there was not enough water around the baby and that I needed to be induced. I cried because I was instantly scared of the unknown pain that I was about to endure. The labor pains were the absolute worst! Brandon was there to help to some extent but that was short lived. In the middle of me having these excruciating contractions he was on the couch taking a nap. Thank God for his mother. She had become a 2nd mother to me. My mother was not able to be there for the birth of my daughter, but Brandon's mom filled in during my labor. She held my hand during my labor pains, while her son slept on the couch. She was not happy about that at all. I literally had to go to the bathroom about 20 times the night they induced me. She walked with me every time without complaining. During this time of our relationship Brandon wasn't really who had shown me he was in the beginning. He changed. I remember yelling from being in so much pain and agony, and he woke up out his sleep and said, "can you be quiet, I can't sleep". His mother almost knocked him out. That night of labor was rough so the doctors gave me meds so that I could sleep. The next day his mom went home to go shower and change and came back just in time. It was time to push! It wasn't the easiest birth, but God was there all the way. I remember the baby's heart rate dropped and about 5 doctors rushed in with concern. By then, my grandmother was there and everyone was on their best behavior. I didn't panic. I prayed. For some reason I wasn't scared, I don't know if it is because it didn't register to me that my baby was in danger or what. Nonetheless, we had a safe delivery. Seeing my newborn's face was love at first sight. All the pain that I had endured, I instantly forgot. I remember everyone holding her and when she got to Brandon's mom, it hit me that it was HER BIRTHDAY. I looked at her and said, "happy birthday". She said "OMG, it IS my birthday". I don't believe she realized it was her birthday until that very moment. She is so selfless and focused on me that it didn't occur to her that it was her birthday. Brandon's mother has been there for me since I was 19 years old. She wasn't too eager to meet me or initially get to know me. She figured we were young and more than likely we weren't going to be but so serious at our age, at least this is what Brandon told me when we first made it official. She had no clue that I would end up being the daughter that she never had but always wanted. Our first New Year's Eve we spent together at church. I knew that I would meet his mom that day but I had no plans on how we would connect. I can't remember exactly what the Pastor preached this night, but whatever it was, it woke up every bottled up emotion in me. I completely broke down and could not stop crying. I was thinking about my mother and I was so worried about her at the time. All of the hurt that I was feeling poured out like an ocean full of tears. Before I knew it, I was in Brandon's mother's arms. She was a complete stranger to me and there I was crying my eyes out with a running nose in her arms. She would describe me as "snotting and carrying on". LOL. After church we formally met and she was much nicer than Brandon had made it seem that she would be. I think that day she connected with me on a more spiritual level. I am pretty sure after that, Brandon gave her the background on my mother not being around like that, and that may have initiated her opening a soft spot in my heart for me. Soon, she invited me over for dinner and a sleepover. Even Brandon was shocked, he said that his mother has never invited any of his girlfriends over for a sleepover. That night, she made stuffed shrimp, which happens to be one of my favorite meals. She set up movie night for all 3 of us in the basement and we had an amazing time. She told me that I could just call her "Ma-B", which for me was a bit of a tongue twister, I felt like I was saying "mombee". Before I knew it, I was at their house on a regular basis and calling her "mommy". Her home has always been so inviting. Everything is always in place, and it has always felt so warm and full of love, just like her. I learned a lot from her growing up as well. Many people mistake her for my mother and my mother for Brandon's mother. When Brandon and I first got together, people were telling me that I looked like her before I had ever met her. One thing she has always taught me was to always keep myself up no matter what. She is that woman that you will absolutely NEVER catch slipping. She is always on point from head to toe. She has to wear a uniform when she is working, yet every day she manages to get herself dressed to impress, just to take off her outfit when she enters the building. She too is a woman of grace, and a class act at that. When I was pregnant with Marley and walking around looking a mess, she stopped me in my tracks. She told me that I needed to pull it together and take the scarf off my head, and to make sure that I looked cute and pregnant. After she had that brief conversation with me, I made sure that I got up every morning and looked my best. People would tell me all the time that I was one of the cutest pregnant girls that they have ever seen. From the age of 19 on, she has been there to celebrate every milestone in my life. She and "granny" (Brandon's now 92 year old grandmother). God blessed me with an extra mom and grandmother all in one scoop. I could not have even handpicked a better, now, mother-in law for myself. I could never be able to repay her for all that she has done or continues to do for me. Only God could gift her with the most sentimental gift ever, her first grandchild being born on her birthday.

Our first baby being born was a new beginning to us both. This is the part where growing up was necessary and it needed to happen, FAST. The first couple of weeks with Marley being in the world were challenging. There was a lot of love and a lot of arguments. Everything was a challenge for me; the waking up, the crying, the diaper changes, the breastfeeding, and the list goes on. This was the first time in my life that I had to be responsible for someone other than myself. I heard of people speak of post-partum but I didn't realize how real it was until it hit me. It was summertime. During the day Brandon would go out with his friends and enjoy his day and I was left many times with the baby to care for. I was nursing so I barely caught any breaks. The nursing became beyond frustrating to me. I felt like the baby was never full and she cried constantly during the day. One day I was so overwhelmed with motherhood, I remember thinking that I didn't see how a person could hurt a child, but I could see how having a baby could make them loose their mind. I was loosing my mind. Everyday was the same. I would get up, feed the baby, change the baby, hop in the shower once I got her to sleep, and as soon as I got in I would have to get out because she would cry. I would feed her again, change her again, REPEAT, REPEAT, REEEEE-PEAT! There was no change in my schedule other than what I ate for that day or who came to visit. This sent me into a depressed state of mind. When she would cry, I would cry with her. My nipples wore sore as heck and that irritated me even more. I remember telling Brandon,

"I cant breastfeed anymore, it's too much". He snapped, and went on and on about how I wasn't a good mother, and I was weak if I decided to give up on breastfeeding. His words pierced my soul and this was the point where I started to feel like I was being verbally abused. I am not sure if it was us having a baby together that made him feel a comfort in thinking that I wouldn't leave, but this was the start. Arguments got worse. Words got more toxic. It just got bad. It was time that I made a move. I decided to take up my mother's offer and go live with her to gain some peace. My mother offered me and the baby to come stay with her, this was a blessing and right on time. She had a 2-bedroom apartment and told me that one of the rooms was for the baby and I if we ever wanted to stay. I started to get out of the house more as the baby got a little older. I remember being at my mom's apartment and the baby kept crying and I just broke down crying. I told her it was too much! I cried my heart out that day. When Brandon came to pick me up and saw me crying he didn't understand. I got in the car and when he pulled off he said, "What the f##k you crying for"? He had gotten comfortable to being insensitive to my feelings and I was getting more and more tired of his mess. I told him that one day he would look up and me and the baby would be gone. I kept that promise. He begged me not to leave when I packed up all my things from his mother's house. The baby and I moved in with my mom. I had been planning before I actually left. I would spend the night sometimes before completely moving in with her. She smoked in her house when we weren't there and I could smell it on our clothes when we left. I helped her pay to get what was going to

47

be me and Marley's room painted, and to get new carpet to help kill the smell of smoke. I'm so funny when it comes to where I live and my mother was very accommodating on making sure my "living quarters" check off list was complete. When I moved in, it was like one of those HGTV shows had come in and revamped the whole apartment. It was nice before, but it was even nicer after the makeover. I felt so comfortable with my new move and gained more peace. Finally I could relax and map out my future plans.

3 BURNED
IT MAY STING A LITTLE, BUT IT GETS BETTER

Before I continue with how great it was moving in with my mom, I would like to give a background of the relationship that I had with my mother growing up. This is essential to the first experiences of me masking my emotions and having anxiety. This was the first time in years that I had lived with my mother. Living with her was something that I yearned for most of my life. I used to see my friends with their parents and be so jealous of them having their "mommy" at home. Meanwhile, my mom was sometimes nowhere to be found. At school I felt left out. People would ask about my mother and I would lie and say she was at home, work, or wherever decent place I could think of. The reality was, many times I had no idea where she was. During the younger years of my life, I did not know that my mother had a drug addiction. I am not sure if it was the age that made me naïve to the fact or that I was just too blind to see it. I always knew that she was a main part of my life that was missing but I did not know why. The questions of "where is your mom" started at a young age for me and so did the lies that I would make up. To others who did not know who my mother was and what I was going through, I would portray this perfect motherly image of my mother to them. I cried a lot to myself at night thinking about my mother growing up. I am an "I will believe it when I see it" type of person because my trust issues began with my mother. I do not put my full trust into people because most of my life when I believed what my mother said, many times I was let down. I started bottling in my feelings at a very young age. When I was about 5 years old I was waiting on my mother to pick me up from school, it was dark, and all of the kids were gone. The school called the fire department to come to pick me up because they could not get in touch with my mother. I remember sitting there with my book bag on in a chair kicking my feet back and forth and being very quite thinking, "she forgot about me". I never showed any emotions. She eventually came running down the hall and I felt a sense of relief but still very confused. My thoughts as a child were: "I can understand you forget your purse, or maybe your keys, or maybe ANYTHING. But, how do you forget ME!? HOW IN THE WORLD DO YOU FORGET ME. How could you leave me sitting here scared like this? Why didn't you call"? I never told her how I felt. We are who we are as adults because of our experiences as children. Here I am almost 34 years old and I still feel like that child at 5. I still bottle my emotions in the same way I did that day. Sitting, swinging my legs, with a book bag FULL OF EMOTIONS! I have carried my emotions on my back in this imaginary book bag my entire life. My emotions have weighed on me so heavy and caused me to have anxiety about everything, especially things I have no control over. I try to protect my children from having anxiety by never letting them feel the same ways that I have felt. I promised myself that when I had children I would be the best mother that I could possibly be, and I feel that I have outdone myself. If I am ever running late to get my kids I make sure that I call way in advance because, I do not want them to ever think that "I forgot about them". My mom has missed so many important moments in my life. I felt no one could relate to my mom missing out of my life at school, but "around the way" this was normal for many of us. Our entire block was a family. My neighbors were my first friends, cousins, brothers and sisters. Not only did we grow up together, but our parents also grew up together. To go a little further back my GRANDFATHER and my god-brothers GRANDFATHER grew up together. My GREAT-GRANDMOTHER taught my god-brothers grandfather how to read. In a nutshell, our neighborhood had a family tree of its own. Most of us on the block were being raised by our grandparents, while our parents ran the streets. So, around the way it was normal for our parents to be running the streets or "around the corner" aka Kennedy St. Growing up around Kennedy Street in the 80s would either make or break you. The end result of growing up around there was, you make something of yourself, become a drug dealer or drug addict, become an alcoholic, went to jail or got killed. My mother came up in that "crack" era as most of our parents did if you are in your early 30's like me. The difference with me was not my mother coming up in that era, it was her falling victim to the streets of that era. Again, back then I had no idea what was going on. As I got older I started to realize that my mother was a drug addict. I started finding drugs at a young age and did not even realize what it was until I got older. I remember seeing the foils, spoons, glass, bags, and whatever else she used for her addiction but I could not comprehend what those things were. I started to put the pieces together when I was about 11 or 12. I would have flash backs of me finding these very same things along with small zip lock bags the size of the tip of my pinky finger in random places. Once I realized what was going on it made sense that she was not there the way that I needed her. Sometimes I would sneak in her purse to find evidence of empty drug bags that matched her behavior. I started to be able to tell that she was high. As I got older I never accused her of being high I would just say, "Ma did you take some medicine or something, you are acting funny". When people are on drugs they are not who they really are. As an adult I am not angry with my mother, being an addict is a sickness. You always hear "say no to drugs" and it's pretty vague. But, in my head its like NO, NO, NO, NO, NOT EVER TO DRUGS! I have seen and experienced way too much. While my sister and I mainly lived with our grandparents, periodically, we lived with our mother. But, each time our grandparents came back to get us because of her addiction. At the age of 6 or 7 I was forced to grow up. My mother would leave my sister and I in the house by ourselves while she went out and got high. Read that age again! SIX AND SEVEN!! Sometimes she would be gone for 20 minutes, sometimes she was gone for 5 hours. My sister Rence' and I are very, very, very close. For most of our lives, it was just us growing up together. We are only a year and a half a part, but the way that I play the big sister role is like she is 7-10 years younger. My mother being in the streets matured me at an early age. I always had Rence' right behind me to look after. She is the only other person that could relate to my experiences because she was the only one there with me. We have a younger sister that was with us during some of those times, but that relationship was snatched from us, and I will not go into that part of my pain. It was always "Rence':Kiki" not "and Kiki" just one name like I said. We were one and we were raised as one. Now, even though my mother wasn't in her right mind most of my childhood, she has always taught my sister and I that if we didn't have anyone else, at the end of the day we still had each other. When we would get mad at each other she would make us hold hands until our palms got sweaty. Now that I think about it, maybe that is why we hate each other's hands today. We do not like the feel of each other's hands, lol. When my mother would leave us alone in the house, we would sit in the window and sometimes look for hours waiting to see any sign of her. I remember sometimes seeing the sun go down and getting really scared, and as soon as that fear of "omg she isn't coming back" would sink in, I would hear her turning the door. During this time we were living in our family owned apartment building, in South East, D.C. My great-grandfather and uncles purchased that building back in the day, and I was told that they said they wanted to make sure people in our family always had somewhere to live. My mother lived there rent free. When she would leave she would instruct us NOT to open the door for NOBODY or NOTHING. Most of the time we listened. Other times we would just go downstairs to "Aunt Becks" apartment, or to another family member's apartment that lived in the building. I guess my mom felt we were safe there because we had other family members living there. But, as children you just want your "mommy". When our grandparents would catch on to what was going on, they came to our rescue every time. It wasn't stable living with her, so we would move back with them. Now, I have always had my father in my life and my other side of my family, but I wanted to live with my grandparents and my sister. Living with my grandparents was comforting to me because I was there with my first friend most of the time, my sister. As we got older around 10 or 11 my mother's patterns continued. I became immune to her behavior and this was when I started to build a wall up to protect my feelings. I would hear from her when she would get locked up or when she would periodically stop by the house to get money, or to see us. Each time that she would get locked up, I hoped that that time in jail would be the last time, and that she would finally get herself together. I hated going to the jails to see her and putting that dirty phone to my ear to talk to her. I would cry each time that I left. I do not recall ever seeing one picture of myself as a baby or toddler with my mother. I can only remember one picture of her and I with my sisters when I was about 7. There was one picture of my mother and I when I was a baby. You could see me but you could only see her legs. That picture reminds me of the mother on the "Muppets", on that show they never showed the mothers face, only her legs. When she would come to my grandparent's house my sister and I would be so excited! I never wanted her to leave because I always had the fear of not knowing when I would or if I would ever see her again. When she left, she always said she was coming "right back". Most of the time it would be a long time before she came back, sometimes hours, sometimes days, one time I did not hear from her or see her for a whole YEAR. I remember because I counted the days. I hate to say this but, when she would go to jail I was relieved. At least when she was there I knew she was safe and where she was. I was constantly afraid of what may happen to my mother. There was always a constant fear of getting one of the worst calls of my life about her. This fear left me feeling constantly anxious. When she would pop up over our grandparent's house, I always cried when she left. I never wanted her to leave. I remember one day my grandmother said, "You act like you can't live without your mother". I looked at her and said "I can't". This was a concern for my grandmother but at that time of my life that is honestly how I felt. I could NOT LIVE without her. My sister and I lived with our mom consistently for about one year. At the time we were about 12 and 13 and that year was great. She had a steady job, a great boyfriend, a nice apartment, and that was one of the first times that I felt I finally had her the way I always wanted her. She would come home and cook us amazing meals, help us with homework, give us house rules, she was just a regular mom. After a while of being consistent my nightmares of her leaving slowly started to come back. "I'll be right back, I am going to the store. Do not call your grandparents". As an adult when I hear people say "right back" I instantly do not believe them. I make up in my mind that "I will see them when I see them", because my mother has always said that and never meant it. With my sister and I being a little older at the time, the 5 hours max of her being gone when we were younger, sometimes became a day, maybe 2. Some days my sister and I would find ourselves getting ready for school and going to school on our own, with no mother at home. We knew at this age that we were finding drugs for sure. We would scoop up all the evidence and call our grandfather. "Deddy, my mother did not come home. Please don't tell her that we called! Oh, and we found a spoon and this plastic thing with foil". He came to our rescue every time to pick us up. When we got to our grandparent's house the worrying of being left alone was never a concern. My mother had a sense of us calling our grandparents, because it was almost instant that she would call or show up with a new excuse as to why she left us. She always had a story about how she "only" went to the store and was not gone long. I always have struggled with expressing my feelings because I have always hid how I felt about my mom not being there. She missed out on so much. One of the most special moments I recall her missing is me getting ready for prom. It was great to have my grandmother, aunts, cousins, and other women in my family there but not having my mother there really hurt. She promised she would be there, another broken promise. Every special event in my life(leading up to me becoming a mother) I worried if my mother would be there or not, and if she was, if I would be embarrassed. One of the most embarrassing and hurtful days for me was, when I felt that my "secret" of my mother being an addict got out to my school mates. I was on my way to school and I thought I saw my mother, but I wasn't sure. This lady was smaller than me and I was a size 0. I followed her a little just to catch "her" walk, or for her to say something in the distance that I could hear, to confirm that this was NOT my mother's voice. I started to yell "MA" and when I did the lady sped up so I was sure it wasn't her. I continued to walk to the metro. The lady ended up slowing down and I was able to catch up with her. It felt like someone had stabbed me in the heart because it WAS my mother. I was so embarrassed and hurt when I got a closer look. She was way smaller than me and did not look like herself. She looked like a TV "crackhead". I hate that word, I do not call people that, but that is the best way that I could describe what I saw. What I was used to seeing was a mother that was just in and out. I had never seen this look before. My mother had never "looked" like a drug addict to me until this day. She hugged me and it felt like I was hugging air. For whatever reason she wanted to ride the train with me to school. I did not want to sit by her, so I moved away in a close enough distance for her to know that I was there with her, but in a far enough distance for others not to think we were not together. People from my school started to get on the train. I was praying that she did not start talking to me as I watched her periodically "nod" off. She was a heroin addict. As the train got fuller with schoolmates, my heart was beating really fast. My mother came over close to me and laid her head on my shoulders. This was the day that I felt silent whispers around me and it bothered me so bad being in high school. She could tell that I was embarrassed as she slurred and asked me if I was embarrassed. I said, "no, Ma". She kissed me as I got off the train and I cringed. I wanted to burst into tears but, again here I go pouring these emotions in this imaginary book bag as I carried them on my back. I held back my tears and let them sit in my eyes and blur my vision as I walked to school. The older I got, the more embarrassed her actions became. Earlier I stated what people from my neighborhood became as they became adults. One of those things was the guys becoming drug dealers. As I got older some of the guy friends that I had grew up with became the newer generation on the block of drug dealers. I did not ever think that I would be impacted by their lifestyle, but I was. One day one of my childhood friends that chose that life told me that my mother asked him to give her some drugs. He said, "I told Ma, nah", as if I would get some type relief of him being "considerate". I was completely embarrassed. The thoughts rushed through my mind of who else he shared this information with. Growing up there was a song, I am not sure the name of it but I want to say it was, "your mother's on crack rock". In that song there was a little girl being teased and kids were around her singing and chanting, "your mova's on crack rock". The little girl responds and says, "not my mova". When I used to see that video (and other kids that I knew were laughing and mimicking it), I would get so mad inside. I would want to cry because it hurt me that someone would make fun of someone else's pain, especially my pain, but no one knew my pain. Those kids had no idea what I was struggling with. I never verbally said that my mother was a drug addict until one day I could not hold it in any longer. When I was contracting for the government (before quitting to pursue my dream of becoming a hairstylist full time), there was a slight debate in our office. There was a girl talking about someone that she knew of who had turned out to be nothing because her mother was on drugs. I listened to her mouth off saying, "people who have drug addict parents end up being bums. They don't go to college. They drop out of high school and they end up on drugs", her list of all things negative went on. One of the guys in the office was going back and forth with her telling her that in many cases that was not true. She stood strongly about what she said, until I opened my mouth to shut her up while trying to hold back my tears. I said, "that is not true, some people take the negative and turn it into positive". She tried to shut me up by saying, "YES! It IS true. I have never met someone that parents were on drugs and they turned out to not be that way". It was time I shut her down for once and for all. "My mother been on drugs most of my life! She was not around most of my life. I finished high school! I graduated from college! I am a great mother! And I am not any of that of what you just described". Bam! Case closed. She looked at me as if she felt stupid, and I looked at her as if she was for saying such a thing. Everyone in the office got very quiet. It is important to be very careful how you voice your opinion about certain things publically. You have no idea what a person is going through or what they have been through. I was very much offended by her ignorant perception, and at the same time I was very shocked that I had uttered what I said to her. I could not believe that I actually said my mother was "a drug addict". Those words sound so harsh to me, typing it even feels harsh. One thing for sure that I have always known was that was that my mother LOVED ALL 3 of her kids. She always told us, she never hid it, and she was very affectionate, she was just "sick". I do not blame or feel any anger towards my mom for any of her actions. She has her own testimony as to why she was who she was and why she is who she is today. Even with her being a missing piece most of my childhood, I still learned a lot from my mother. I got my "gangster" from my mother. My mother is a straight gangster if there ever was one. I am a very quiet person, but I can transform into Stoney from "Set it Off" real quick. I will set it off! My mother "trained me to go" at a very young age. One day I was waiting for the school bus to come, and this girl that was friends with someone who did not like me kept mouthing off about me. I listened, and stayed quiet, hoping that she stopped. She kept going!! I turned around and probably gave that girl til this day the curse out of her life. I can not remember what I said, but it was a whole lot of b-words, f-u's and whatever else I said to her to shut her up. I left her standing there looking very stupid, I did what she or no one else expected and she never opened her mouth to me again, until I bumped into her as an adult. "Hey, I remember you"! In my head I'm like "yeah but do you remember that cuss out"?! This was learned behavior from my mother that I needed. She taught me street life stuff, you know, survival skills. The things I needed as she would say to "let a m-f-er know". I remember one time I cried to her about this girl that kept picking on me. The girl and I were friends at one point but at this time we weren't anymore. I went on and on to my mother about how she kept messing with me, after we had already been in a fight before. The first time we fought was in my mother's apartment. This was the day I got the best of her, but no one was around but her friends, her sister, and my sister. They outnumbered us, so their fabricated story of me getting beat up won over everyone's opinion. It was still like I lost because everyone believed what they said. My mother was bout sick of her ish when I told her that the bullying was still going on. She told me flat out, "when she gets out of school, you are going to wait for her at the bus stop! And as SOON as she gets her a$$ off of that bus you betta punch her right in the face. And if you don't hit her I am going to BEAT YO A$$ in front of everybody"! This was not a game, my mother was serious. She WAS going to beat me in front of everyone if I did not do as she said. I caught a different bus that day and got home, dropped my book bag off, practiced how I was going to punch her in the face, and headed for the door. Guess who was behind me? My mother. I still had the first fight of me beating her the first time in my head, so I did not prepare. No Vaseline. No tennis shoes. No timbs. Just me, this rock in my hand (that someone said makes you hit harder), and lastly the dumbest thing ever, some heels. What in thee h-e-double hockey stick WAS I THINKING. I will never forget them ugly heels. They were brown, with shoestrings, and a horseshoe heel. They basically looked like high top bowling shoes. Them things echoed as I walked up to where she would be getting off the bus. My heart was beating so loud and fast. When I got close to her all I remember saying is was, "B-iiiiii-ttttt---c-##" in slow motion. Then I swung on her, and I M-F-N MISSED!!! I MISSED! I swung myself down the hill. Literally! I punched the air and the gravity pulled me to roll down the hill. As I rolled she was running behind me! That winch jumped ON MY BACK and started to beat me all in my face like a monkey!! Her weight was so heavy on me that I could not get up, I thought I was about to die from suffocation. My mother had to come, get some licks in, and pull her off of me. Oh yeah, one of my shoe-boot-tennis-heels came off. I walked the sidewalk of shame back with one shoe missing and a white sweat sock. Bammer! LOL. Bay-bee, they talked about that fight all school year. Even the little boyfriend I had at the time called me and said, "Yeah, I heard you got beat up". I thank God this went down before social media because they probably would have remixed that with Shirley Ceaser's "I got greens, beans, tomatoes, potatoes" however that thing goes. They would have showed me falling 5 times before I actually fell. It was Gods grace that saved me by letting that happen in the 90s and not in this age where it would have went viral that same night. LOL. My mother taught me streets smarts. I needed these traits of her in my survival kit to life. Fall 9 times stand up 10. My mother is living proof of that. She has fell many times, but she is now standing stronger than ever. She has had her struggles, but her struggles are what made her. My struggles have made me. My mother is my right hand now. She is the one that I know is going to have my back and my front. I know that I can call when there is trouble or even if I don't feel well. When she comes over or when I go to her house she caters to me. At 33 years old she will rub my feet until I fall asleep. She loves to cook. I don't care what time of the day or morning it is, if I tell her I am hungry she is going to make sure she makes me something. Most of my life the roles for us have been switched, I have taken on the mother role on many occasions. Many times, taking that role has really weighed heavy on me. Other times, I have felt like a proud parent. One of my proud parent moments was the day she walked across stage from graduating from culinary arts school. I wanted her to look her best on her big day, so I went out and bought her everything she needed from head to toe. I stood in the audience like a proud parent when she crossed the stage. Alexa, play "Hey Mama", by Kanye. "Hey mama, I wanna scream so loud for you cuz I'm so proud of you"! You can't tell me God isn't real. I have seen with my own two eyes what he is capable of doing. My mother has played an essential part in my business growing. She has helped keep my ship a float by creating order and steady flow in my salon. Clients love my mother. She still has no filter, but I have learned that she is who she is and that's just that. She may have missed out on a lot in my life but what matters to me most is that she is here now. She is there when I need her. She is only a phone call away, and further more she is an amazing grandmother to my children. They love them some "Gramma Tammy". She is the crazy grandmother and my kids get a kick out of that. I can exhale to the fact that my "baby" has grown up and she doesn't need me to hold her hand every step of the way. I don't sit up at night worrying about her anymore. Now, I can take a seat back in the seat that was mine in the first place, the daughter's seat.

My father was always around in my life. I lived with my father for a short period of time. My cousins, aunts, uncles and I all went to school together. We were deep. There were about 10 of us all in school together at the same time. He was always very loving and affectionate to me as a young child. The first man to buy me roses was my father. I lived with him until my mom came to pick me up from school and said we were going somewhere. I asked was I going back to my fathers, she said "not right now". I did not realize that she was coming to take me back. I didn't even have the chance to digest what was going on. I could not understand why she was taking me, her issue with him should not have left me in the middle. I don't ever even remember him raising his voice at me. In my eyes my father was a good father. He wasn't missing, he was never locked up, he wasn't ever where I could not reach him, he called, he picked me up, he did not smoke, he did not drink, and he was there consistently. My father even still has some of my childhood memorable items. He has one of my first teddy bears, my first Muslim doll (he is Muslim), my first dress, and tons of pictures of us together. I have definite memories of my father as a child. I remember him doing my hair all the time and he was good at it. We would go places and do things together all the time. I never felt the physical void of my father. He would pick me up most weekends when I was younger, and I could not wait to get over there with my cousins. My father's side of the family has always been the fun side, I mean "fun" fun. I have hundreds, probably thousands of cousins on that side of the family so it has always been a party. My grandmother's house was the house where it was perfectly ok to pop up. You never knew who you would see when you would go over there and you never know who you will see when you go over there now. When we would go over to my grandmother's there would be food, music, jokes, and just us making memories. I can still reflect on these times because she still has VHS videos of us dancing, singing, "jonin" (DC slang for roasting someone), and having a good time. Most of my life Rence' and I shared everything. The one thing that we did not biologically share was my father. When my father would to come get me I would cry for Rence' when he would pull off. It was like a part of me was missing. He would tell me that she can come next time and I would just sit quiet and look sad. We would go some distance before he would make a random U-turn and go back to get Rence'. He would go back to my grandparent's house and say, "come on, get your stuff". Sometimes he would send me in to get her and I was ready like super woman to say his lines, "come on, get your stuff. You coming with us"!! From then on, when I went over, Rence' came too. For as long as I can remember Rence' called my father "Fava" too. I wasn't allowed to call him daddy, he called his father "fava" and I call him the same. Rence' was his daughter too. There has never been a separation. My father is one of the most serious yet funniest people I know. He is not the one to play with unless he says its time to play. Growing up I have always had a fear of my father. I feel like you should have some type of fear of your parents to keep up with the respect for them, but also not such a fear that you can't express yourself. If I did something and someone said "I am going to tell your father", OMG that would be the end of the world for me. I would get serious anxiety and be scared. It wasn't of thinking I was going to get a beaten, it was just of him period. I only remember one beaten from my father, I don't know if that's because over all I stayed on my best behavior or what. But with the one that I did get, I consider myself very lucky that I did not get a beaten any other time. I guess that one was all it took for me. Before the days of him picking up both Rence' and I, when my father would drop me off back home with my grandparents I would cry. I do not know why, but I did most of the times. He would ask me why I am crying and I could never give him an answer, I would just keep crying. When I would get in the house I didn't want to speak to anyone. I would just shut down. My grandfather still says, "We couldn't figure out what was wrong with you. It's like you came back a different person and had to be reprogrammed". As I got a little older and became a teenager, I still went to my fathers but not as often. I was a teenager and had a social life and would spend time with my friends a lot at their house or mine. My father started saying that I was grown at a very young age, not grown as in fast, but grown as in independent. I remember arguments between he, my mother, and grandparents and them saying "she is NOT grown, she is still a child". On my fathers side of the family, things were different, it seems like everyone grew up at a faster rate than on my mothers side of the family. There were a lot of teenage pregnancies. My grandmother had 3 kids by the time she was 18, so I guess in his eyes the estimation of what was grown was different. I would still see him but not as often, and this was not because he did not want to see me, many times I just was in my own teenage world. I started working at the age of 14 and with my job I worked most weekends. On my free time I would have plans every chance I could get with my friends so I had a "busy" teenage life. During my teenage years, I feel like my father let

63

go of my hand. Yes, he was and still is my father, but I have always felt I was missing emotional support and encouragement from him. My love language is words of affirmation and I didn't get too much of that from my father. I was always waiting patiently for him to say something encouraging to me, even as simple as "I am proud of you". I have heard him say that he was proud, but I can almost count the times that he has said that. Deep down I know that he is proud but I just never got too many verbal confirmations. My relationship with my father as I got older has always been a little weird to me. It was never that TV relationship that I would see where a girl would run to her father and jump on him saying "Daddy I love you". There were never random "I love you's", when we did say it, there would be an "appropriate" time to say it. I was very shy around my father, I still am. It's like he knows me but not the real me sometimes. Around him I am the filtered Rickia. I'm not going to say exactly what I am thinking or how I feel. I am not going to walk around singing all loud and giving a Beyoncé show. He has never seen me really dance and I love to dance. If he had been there to hold my hand and give me the emotional support that I needed, I may have been able to cope a little better with my mom missing. It's like when I was around him I had to put my strong mask on. I am ok, I am fine. One of his favorite words is "man". He calls everyone "man". "Man I need to talk to you". "What's your problem man"? Too much "man" for me. I absolutely hate that. I hate it so much that one time a guy called me man and I snapped and cursed him out. I told him to never call me that again. My voice even changes when I talk to my father. Only my sister notices it. It deepens. IT "mans" up. I feel like I am so hard around him, like I can never be the soft person that I am. Hugs sometimes feel awkward and I don't know why. Responding to "I love you" does sometimes as well. I could never explain why. It was not always like this, this is why I say I feel like he let go of my hand too soon. I don't remember feeling this way in my younger childhood years. When it was time for prom, I missed my father being there to see me off as well. I do not remember all that were there or all that were not there. The only two I can clearly remember not being there was my mother and father. When it was time for me to start applying for college his advice was, "Man you don't need to college, just get you a government job and a apartment". In my mind I was confused like, "why would he want me to do that"? It was even hard for me to get some of the things that I needed from him to get financial aid, so a lot of signatures I forged to get to where I was trying to be and that was college. I have never felt like I have had "daddy issues". All my life he has said, "you don't have to live there with your grandparents. You know that. You can always live with me". I never took him up on that offer until I got older. He had a 2-bedroom apartment and I think my grandmother and I weren't seeing eye to eye. I can't remember the exact age that I was, but it was the age where I felt like I could make my own decision and I wanted to be out of my grandparent's house. I walked through my father's house and stared in his prayer room and imagined it being mine. I hinted that I wanted to stay there by saying, "I can just come live with you". I could predict his response because all my life he told me I could live with him. My predictions were wrong. He said, "you can't stay here, ain't no room for you to live here". That day, I felt like I had nowhere to turn but to my grandparents. My mother was still running the streets and the one parent that I thought would welcome me to his home with open arms, did not. I left his house feeling alone and hurt by his words. The thing with words is, they are so sticky. Replaying that day in my head and what he said back then still makes me feel today, exactly how I did that day. It's so true, you never forget how hurtful words make you feel. Whoever made up that "sticks and stones" jingle, must not have ever been hurt by words. They hurt far more than sticks and stones. Words ARE the sticks and stones. Many times the person that says the hurtful things do not remember what they said. You can not be so careless with your words, you must be careful with them. We all have said hurtful things. I am guilty of doing so, we are human, and we aren't made to be perfect. My father showed me what he was taught. It's not that he didn't want the best for me. I just think that growing up this is what he saw; you graduated high school, got a job, and got an apartment. I know that he loves me, sometimes I think I just don't comprehend the way he expresses it. As I stated before, my love language is words of affirmation, I need to be told loving things. His love language may be "acts of services". My father is very catering. He loves to cook, do surprise gestures, and spend time with me. When it comes to materialistic things my father has always made sure I have had the best of the best!! I get my coolness from my father. He is super cool. He is a great interior decorator, I definitely picked this talent up from him. I love to give surprises, just like my father. I love to show my father off, he is a very handsome man and he doesn't look his age at all. He is an amazing grandfather to my children. What I admire most about the relationship he has with my daughter is how close they are. My daughter softens him. She has no problem telling him how she feels. One day she said to him, "Grandfather, you know, you really hurt my feelings". He apologized and told me that he didn't know she was so sensitive. I think with my father, once he knows how sensitive you are, he is more careful with what he says and does. Maybe I should have spoke up a little more growing up, but I never felt as comfortable or as free as my daughter. Over all, as a child I just needed my father to hold my hand a little longer, be a littler softer, more supportive, and more encouraging. Granted I may have missed some of these things from him, but these very same things that I missed helped me push to be who I am now. My father is a very calm person just like me, it takes a lot to get us mad. We are both Taurus's. We really have to be pushed to the limit sometimes to get a reaction. Many people associate Taurus's with being stubborn. I must admit, I am one of the most stubborn people that I know, I am sure that I get this trait from my father because he is as well. One time my father and I were not talking. I cannot remember why he wasn't talking to me, which shows how small it was, but for about a year we had not talked. I would go past his house and leave father's day or birthday cards, and never got a response. When I called, he would not answer. I was ready to just give up on trying, the only reason I was trying was because he was my father. One day during this time, I got one of the scariest calls of my life! My father had been in a fire and was burned pretty bad. My heart was on the floor. I could not get to the hospital fast enough. When I got there, he was wrapped in bandages all over. He had got burned pretty badly, I could not stomach looking at him like this. My father has always been "Pretty Ricky" so seeing him like that was very hurtful. He has always been a nice dresser and been up on the latest. Even now, no one believes that my father is my father. When I was in school my friends would always be shocked! They would joke around and say "Girl, that is your FATHER!? I want to be your stepmother". Those jokes would piss me off. Seeing him laid in that hospital bed like that made us both realize that whatever reason we were not talking was not worth it at all. I feel like my father has toughened me to put my "strong" on. Somehow, I am always able to grab my invisible super girl cape and go off to handle whatever life throws at me. I don't look for people to encourage me, I push myself. I am able to "man" up in life. Maybe, just maybe, I am a magician. I seem to turn a lot of negative things that I have been through in life into something positive. I love my father, and I truly thank him for being all that he has been to me and further more all that he is to my children.

Now that I have given you background information of my parents and my relationships, we pick back up at where we left off. I finally decided it was time that I pack the baby up and move out of Brandon's mom's house, and in with my mom.

4 BREAKAGE
WE ARE NOT GETTING ANYWHERE

I thank God that my mother had her life in order when I had my
daughter. When I left Brandon's moms house, going to my
mother's house was just what I needed to rebuild our mother-
daughter relationship. I had a sense of "home" again. During this
time my mother was one of my biggest support systems. She
cooked the best meals for me, helped with the baby, gave me
encouraging words, and was there to cater to my every need. All
the things that she had been through before was a prerequisite for
the amazing mother and grandmother that she has now become.
Life was good living with my mother. She was the medicine that I
needed to get through the break-up. For the first time in life I
could exhale the relief of having a mother! A mother is the
medicine to their child, even if that medicine comes with side
effects. In the end her being my medicine has contributed to who I
am today, even the side effects of her downfalls helped mold me. It
was me, Marley and my mother living cozy together. Of course
Brandon attempted to get his family back, but I wasn't ready. I

needed to see more changes. During that time, I learned to focus on me more. Most of our relationship I was always waiting hand and foot on him. His life was not centered around mine. My life was centered around his. I would only do things with my friends when I was not with him, because he was with his friends. I did not have too much of a life outside of him. If his friends were to call him and ask him to hang out, he would go at the drop of a dime. I was the complete opposite, I would cancel on my friends to be with him. His mother noticed that I was being walked over and suggested that I read a book entitled "Why Men Love B!tches". After reading that book, I realized that I was too nice. The book talks about how the "nice girl" gets walked over and taken advantage of, while the B!TC# (aka the woman that stands up for herself) is more wanted, attractive and respected. Reading that book helped me so much. I was able to clearly see where things went wrong. I let him get too comfortable. He was so attentive, romantic, and respectful in the beginning. He stopped being who he was in the beginning because I allowed the space for him to get too comfortable. In the beginning of our relationship, he still had to chase me. Guys like a challenge and that is what made him stay on his toes. I was hard to get in the beginning. I messed up by not keeping that same energy. To get him back on his toes during that break up, I had to get the ball back in my court again, and I did. I stopped answering his calls as much and I stopped quickly responding to his texts. When he would call me and think we were about to have a long conversation, I would cut him off with something that made him question if that thing was more important to me than him. I think I even used an example from the book. He called one day and I told him that I was busy organizing Tupper ware, he even questioned me "Tupper ware? That can't wait"? Nope. It could not. When he would come see to get the baby, I sometimes even made sure I wasn't there, and if I was I made sure I was looking cute and unbothered. I dusted off my "little black book" and kept myself busy by entertaining people that I saw no future with, just to keep my mind off of him. He worked his butt off to get us back, and I finally gave in. He finally learned his lesson, right? Wrong! Little did I know, the changes that I needed to see in him would take years and the moving out would become a pattern that continued for us both. We ended up back together and getting a new apartment together and starting a fresh of many starts. When things were good with us they were VERY good and when they were bad, they were VERY bad. We celebrated the good over the years and worked past the bad. So much happened over the years. We got locked up together. Yes, I spent ONE NIGHT in jail. Worst and most confusing night of my life. We were on the way to pick our daughter up from school and got pulled over. This illegal search led them to finding weed in the car and locking us both up. It just so happened as they were putting cuffs on me, my cousin happened to be driving down the street. She spotted me and yelled, "Rickia! Wtf is going on"? I had to talk fast because they were putting me in the police car. I was able to tell her to pick up my daughter. That wasn't nobody but God. What were the chances of me seeing my cousin right on time like that? If I didn't see her my baby would have been at school

72

with no one to pick her up because we could not make any phone calls. The whole ride to the police station I could not believe this was happening. When we got to the station the officers kept saying that I would be released soon. They put me in a room by myself with a window about the size of this book. Immediately my anxiety kicked in, I started to have a panic attack! My chest started to tighten, hands began to shake, and throat felt like it was closing. I started screaming and banging on the door. When the officer opened the door, I was talking so fast in a panic! "Sir! PLEASE! PLEASE! Can I please go where there are bars? I have anxiety and I am freaking out in here! I feel like I can not breathe!" Thank GOD he was generous enough to take me to a cell that made me less anxious. They placed me in a cell right across from Brandon. I tried to keep my calm but I was pissed! He kept saying, "I love you, it's going to be ok. You are going to get out of here." It was summer time, I had on summer clothes and it was FREEZING COLD in that cell. He was able to take off his socks and toss them to me to help keep my feet warm. My mind was going 100 miles an hour. Where is my baby? Is she ok? What is my family thinking? Finally I heard a familiar voice, it was my mother. I thought it was my time to go when the officer came to my cell. Did I mention that my mother is also Super Woman? She is always able to figure out a situation. The officer handed me a brand new velvet sweat suit and said, "your mother just dropped this off for you, she said she knew you would be cold". Let me tell you, her bringing me that sweat suit in that freezing cold cell made up for any Christmas she had ever missed. She had been to jail more than enough to know that I was going to be cold as soon as I got there. I looked at Brandon and told him he better make sure I got out of there! And I was NOT playing. A while after my mother left, I overheard the officers talking. "We taking her to central? I heard they got big rats down there and roaches", they laughed. I was in my head thinking, "This is a joke right"? I thought they were letting me out when they came to my cell, until they said, "come on, you are going to central". Omg I could have died in that moment. I was losing my mind. I was going to spend the night in jail! The whole ride there, I thought about the big rats and roaches that the officers were speaking of. It was me and about 5 other girls in the back of a patty wagon. All of our hands were tied with them plastic handcuff things. These girls were straight savages. You can tell they were heavy in the streets. They cursed each other out (they did not even know each other) and they even cursed the officers out. I was just shaking my head inside like "I wish they shut the h3ll up for we all suffer the consequences". These girls were the type that you would see on scared straight, the ones they would use to scare the girls that came to the jail. Was I scared of any of them? Nope, not at all. Remember my mother trained me to go. I was mentally prepared to spend more time there if one of them tried me. One thing I have never been and that's a sucker. Win or lose, I'm coming up or going down fighting. If my mother had not trained me early on to be sucker-free, I would have been a target. I didn't say much, but my face said it all. My face said, "don't poke the bear". It was survival mode at that point. The whole ride I seriously could not believe what was happening. They took a mug shot, so I knew it was real. When the man took it he said, "you look like you don't belong here" and I quickly told him, "I don't"! When we were walking the halls to our cells, which looked like animal cages, it was dark and scary. I did not know what to expect. All I heard was a bunch of banging and everyone shouting various demands to whoever "C-O" was.

"C-O Bring me some fu$k#ng water"!!!

"C-O, what time we eat"!?

"C-O, this b!t#h is going to make me kill her, you may want to get her out of my cell"!

I later found out when I got released that "C-O" meant correctional officer. It was really like a scene out of a movie. It was like entering a wild zoo. When I got in my cell and they locked the door that was it. I was really there, and I had no idea when I was leaving. I said a prayer and asked God to cover me and to keep me calm so that I would not have an anxiety attack. The girl that was in my room appeared to be either a prostitute or a drug addict. She was a white girl. She gave me 8 Mile vibes. The bunks look just like cookie sheets, they were metal and hard. No pillows, no sheets, no blanket, no nothing. There was a dirty toilet in the room and when we had to go to the bathroom there was no privacy. I held my pee as long as I could until I could not any longer. When I finally went, I was trying to hide as much of my butt as I could. There was barely any tissue and they weren't giving any out, I had to wipe with about 3 squares. This was the nastiest experience that I could imagine. You could hear people ask what time it was and that's the only way I was able to estimate the time. I would talk to myself, "okay so I heard someone ask for the time an hour ago and it was 10:20 then, so it probably is about 11:30 now ". Soon after I answered my own question, someone else had asked what time it was and this was exactly an hour later according to my calculations. Do you know it was TEN THIRTY FIVE a whole HOUR later!? *Throws hands up like Kevin Hard "NIIIIIIII-GUUUUHHH"* Let me tell ya'll life is only on speed ball out here. In jail, I think they are on B.C. time. If you want to be off your Maxine Waters blast and "reclaim your time"! Go to jail. I am going to have to Google "jail conversion time", for every 10 hours out here it must be 10 minutes jail time. So, correction, I spent one night of free people time, but 2 weeks of jail time when I got arrested. It's like "crack the window and let some time in this joint"! I never ate the lame sandwiches they passed around that night and I refused food and water. I thought it couldn't get worse, I was tripping. The next morning we had to go to court to meet with lawyers. That wait was even longer, but we were all in one room and not chained up. Females were in there arguing, about to fight, and talking about what they were going to do when they got out. They were talking about getting out and going BACK to where they were when they got locked up. I made up in my head they were crazy. There was a toilet there where we had to go in front of each other also. There was a little more privacy, but not much. Women were on their cycles and the "C-O's" weren't giving them any sanitary napkins. It was just nasty. One girl said to me just like the officer did when I got checked in, "you don't even look like you belong here". I gave her and whoever the background of why I did not belong there. "No, I don't. This has nothing to do with me. I am a mother. I am a college graduate. I work for the government. I have never been locked up before", and whatever else I said that sounded like "Miss Goodie-2-shoes". All of them said, "Oh yeah you going to get no papered". They were all unlicensed lawyers. This was not their first (and from the conversations that they had it wasn't their last) time being in jail. There was one girl there that I was able to relate to because her lifestyle was very parallel to mine. She and I talked the rest of the time and that made time go by. We all spent about 12 hours in that one room with no food or water, you don't get those "luxuries" at the court building. I got "no papered" and they let me out that night. Most people like to brag that they got locked up or went to jail. Shoot, not me, for most people that are reading this that know me, this is their first time getting word of this. When I got out, my mother was the first person waiting for me. "MAAAAAAAAA"!!! I went on and on for hours about my experience and that was nothing to her. I had forgot that I was talking to the "locked up queen" herself. The way she talked about her jail experiences you would have thought she was on a resort. I remember one time when I went to visit her in jail her whole face was beat down honey. I'm looking around for the Mac counter and whole time baby girl had did that face with pencils and melted crayons. What in the H#LL!? LMAO. So, yeah, she pretty much cracked up at my experience and kept looking for more for me to tell her. "What else Ki"? She was asking questions with a smile on her face like I was doing a comedy show and she was anticipating my next joke. Brandon spent much more time than I did there, I was afraid of his outcome. I prayed on it, he was eventually released and we put that situation behind us. We were doing really well after that, things were looking up. He came back correct this time and proposed to me. This was the FIRST engagement. The first time that he proposed was at the Miami airport as we were on our way home from vacation. He kept saying that his stomach was hurting, I sat and waited while he texted me from the bathroom. Then he texted me asking for me to come towards the bathroom because the police was right there and they were calling the ambulance. When I got there and saw the police standing over him, I was scared. Brandon was on the floor with his body balled up and holding his stomach crying. I panicked and went to bend down to grab him and as I did, he started crying (real tears) and said; "I love you so much! I really do! Would you please marry me"? I was shocked when he pulled out the ring and I said, "YES" with tears in my eyes. People in the airport stopped in their tracks to bask in our moment. Everyone was clapping and congratulating us. This was it. The moment that I had been waiting for finally came! Right? WRONG! We stayed engaged for about 5 years. We started planning the wedding and later stopped because neither one of us were ready. We had bigger blow ups, tons of arguments and the list goes on. He was back to being comfortable, I allowed the space for him to get back there again. We would get into some very heated arguments, and I would get physical. One time when he was sleep I went through his phone and saw some very questionable things. Instead of me waking him up with a tap on his shoulder, I marched in the room with keys in my hand and my fist balled up. I banged him in his face like that pop up hippo game at Chuck E. Cheese! He jumped up out of his sleep in a state of confusion and panic yelling, "WHAT THE H#LL IS WRONG WITH YOU!? WHY WOULD YOU HIT ME LIKE THAT"? I have no idea why I hit him in his sleep, he could have really gotten hurt. I was dead wrong for that. Thank God he never hit me. He took the high road, and I am blessed that he did because he could have really hurt me. Our home became crazy! We would argue, tussle, break things, have the neighbors call the police, and so on. Our home environment was very toxic for us all. The most hurtful part about these things is our daughter witnessed a lot and she was now old enough to start remembering. She would scream and cry frantically when it would get that bad. If I could take anything back it would be those images. Images of me hitting her father, him calling me names, just us conducting ourselves like two wild animals. One time he got so mad that he ripped a picture of the 3 of us that was on the wall, off! She started crying a cry that I had never heard and this is when I knew it was time to change!! Before it was different, she was younger and at an age where she was too young to remember, and it wasn't ever as bad as it had gotten. Now, she was at the age where she would remember these events and remind me of them later. "You remember when daddy took down our picture and broke it"? Her asking these types of questions broke my heart. Children are very impressionable and adult behavior is learned behavior from childhood. I had many anger issues as a child that I kept bottled in, I did not know how to talk much, I just knew how to fight. As an adult this became a bigger issue. I should not ever result to putting my hands on anyone. This was not my last time snapping the way I did that night. I could go on and on and on to you about stories. One time he decided to jump on the hood of my car in hopes that I would not pull off. Wishful thinking, skurrrtt. I took off with him on the hood until he decided it was best that he jumped off. Another time I got so mad with him that I walked to his car and acted like I had something to tell him so that he could roll the window down. Once he cracked it a little, I sprayed pepper spray inside and he had no idea what I did so he quickly rolled the window up. I walked back to my car and sat and watched him choke from the spray. He was bringing out every piece of evil in me from his actions. At this point, we both were crazy because we still ended up back together.

Six years after we had our daughter we were expecting our son. This was the son that we prayed for and also the son that he promised if God blessed us with, he would stop going out as much. I felt like I was giving, giving, giving and not getting my needs met in return. Two kids later, still not married, still dealing with disrespect, still immature, and still playing games. We had a schedule and part of that schedule consisted of him packing his things about once every other month. When I say packing I don't mean a gym bag and some shoes. I mean boxes, bags, shoeboxes, and clothes still on the hangers. Now that I think about it he could have started a moving company as fast as he was with packing his things. One day I told him that the next time that he decided to pack his things he would have to take them and leave, for good. One day my mother happened to enter the "packing party", his things were out the closet and boxes of shoes were stacked to the ceiling. He had them sitting there for days, if not a week. She saw that all his things were packed again and she said, "Son, put your stuff up, come on now ya'll always do this. You aren't going anywhere". He had a smirk on his face, I guess him knowing the drill he was a little embarrassed that she called us out. She attempted to put his things back in the closet. This time was different. Any other time I would help him reorganize. I said, "No". I told Brandon the next time that he packs his things he has to leave". For the first time ever, I felt the seriousness in my voice. Me being the "lingering" friend resulted in me sticking around and dealing with the same things over and over and over again. But once I am done I will "erase you like I drew you". I was at the point that I was tired of venting to my friends and family. Sometimes, like in my case, the best thing a person's friends and family can do is, just listen. Granted I wasn't dealing with the amount of verbal abuse that I was before, but it would still happen occasionally, and when it did it was really bad. After a while I got tired of hearing myself talk. I was tired of hearing silence on the other end of the phone of whoever I was venting to. My friends and family stopped giving me the advice that I was not taking. Our relationship had not only become draining to us, but it was to the people who loved and cared about us as well. What I learned in this experience is, it doesn't matter how much advice you give a person, people leave when THEY are tired, not when EVERYONE else is. The fear of me waking up one day and being in my 40s and still going through the same hit me. This was not what I wanted for my life. I did not want to miss out on the husband God had for me for the husband I was trying to make for myself. I hit a growth spurt and that required me to change myself first and then any toxic environments that I was in. I know that I have fallen short in areas during our relationship and I take full ownership of my downfalls. However, I feel like every action of mine was a reaction to all that he was putting me through.

Before leaving, for what I thought was for good, it was time for me to mentally check out of the relationship before I physically did. It all started with a spiritual cleansing. I needed God. It was time to pray like never before. I started going to church a lot to clear my mind. I needed the strength to leave what was all so familiar to me. It was scary. What if I don't find the husband I am looking for? What if he moves on before I do? How am I going to feel about another woman around my kids? All of these feelings poured on me like I was in the middle of a storm with no umbrella, as I cried. It's one thing to be raining, but it's another thing for it to be raining and you are crying. I have cried some of my best cries in the rain, literally. I hate crying and I hate letting people see me cry. But, something about me crying in the rain makes me feel like I'm not really crying. Almost as if I am just blending in with the rain, and at the time I felt so out of touch with the world it was like I was happy to be a part of the rain. Rainy days were made for crying in my world. People in traffic couldn't tell. My kids couldn't tell. I would just blend in with the rain. My feelings, my tears, the rain and I were the perfect storm. A storm that was would soon pass, with a lot a prayer. My prayer was very specific "God give me the feelings I need to get through whatever I need to go through". I stopped praying for his words and actions to diminish, I just wanted to detach myself from the way his words and actions made me feel. That is a continued prayer for me in every aspect of my life even still. I would say to myself, "God just teach me how to dance in the rain. I just need to know that you are there when it starts to pour down". I remember listening to a TD Jakes podcast and he said, "You wouldn't need a washer machine if you didn't have dirty clothes, with adversity comes opportunity". There is no sunshine without rain. Although I didn't want to hear "time heals all wounds", it was true. It was hard initially to be in a house with someone who was not there physically or the way that I needed him to be emotionally. It took years for me to get mental peace. I used to be scared to say, "God reveal the truth" because I was scared of how I may FEEL once the truth was revealed. I changed my prayer to asking God not only to reveal the truth, but to also grant me the feelings to be able to handle whatever the truth was. I had to seek God for the strength. I needed to stop talking and venting to my friends and call on him. One day I woke up and I promise you it was like I had no feelings. That is just how God works. I could not believe how numb I was feeling. God answered my prayers and removed me mentally from the situation that was draining me for years. I stood at that very same hallway looking down the stairs, and flashbacked to where Brandon stood when he told me to "s##k his d##k" in front of our daughter, and I felt completely numb. He didn't come home the night before and I did not care. Me blowing up his phone 40 and 50 times stopped. The texts with me asking him where was he, completely stopped. Asking him to spend time with me stopped. It all just stopped one day. It did not happen overnight but ONE day it in all went into effect. I had an inner peace that could not be compromised due to my circumstances. I had mentally checked out of the verbally abusive relationship that I was in. Verbal abuse is just as bad as physical. It's all abuse and it is NOT OK. I was tired of being abused by his words. I was tired of giving him everything that he wanted and me not getting what I felt like I deserved, a marriage. To Brandon marriage was just a sheet of paper that could wait. So was money, you think he was waiting on a check or going to chase it? Everything I did for him I did in hopes that he would change. I always kept the house looking good, hoping that he would want to stay home. I moved us out further away from the city, thinking he would love it and want to spend all his time out there with me. God blessed me with the son that he promised, "if you give me a son I promise I am just going to be home with him all the time! Please just give me a little man". None of these things changed his behavior. Yeah for a little while he would be in the house cooking, cleaning, rubbing my belly, helping with Marley and doing what he was supposed to do. Even after our son was born he stayed on his job. But, soon after the newness of the baby wore off, he was back

to his antics of being disrespectful and immature. Don't get me
wrong; he has always been a provider. He has always made sure his
kids and I were good. They have always had what they wanted and
definitely what they needed. That alone should be more than
enough right? I'm sorry boo, that was not the case for me. Okay
you are paying the bills, but I am here alone most days. Okay you
take care of your kids, but most of the time it's just the kids and
me. I have had pretty much anything that I have wanted
materialistically. But, I am not a materialistic woman so those
things do not make me happy. I would much rather be in a one-
bedroom apartment with he and my kids and be happy, than being
in something more luxury with tons of space with them and being
miserable. I just wanted peace. Once God granted me the feelings I
needed to maneuver through the mess I was in, peace instantly
followed. I had inner peace and I could not ask for anything more.
Inner peace goes with you everywhere, it is not based on your
circumstances. Inner peace will have you able to master being able
to tune out chaos around you. Inner peace makes you feel good!
With this good ole peace in my life, I started going to work with a
new spirit. There was no more crying at the trashcan. The talks my
mother would have with me finally sank in. "Girl do you know
who you are? You are the bomb! You need to know what your
hand calls for"? I finally figured it was time that I start to move and
live my best life. There was a new me to come, and the new me
wasn't taking any shorts.

5 NEW CLIENT
NEW MAN, WHO DIS?

It was a warm October, I would never forget the day because I remember talking a cute selfie after I got "Peter's" number. I was minding my business walking to my car after leaving the salon. He walked over to my car and said, "You are so beautiful, I would love to take you out one day". So turned on by the fact that he walked over to the car and didn't beep the horn, I gave him my number. Looking back now I am cracking up to myself thinking, "Really Ki? Girl you were so vulnerable". Now this was actually the second turn on for me. I said, "This must be God" because I had met him a year before the EXACT same month. I remembered walking out the salon with my newborn son. He approached me and said, "Are you still with your child's father"? I said, "yes". He said, "Ok well you have a nice day". Back then, I admired the fact that he didn't try to continue to talk to me by hitting me with that stupid 90s "You can't have friend's" line. As I pulled off from the second encounter (that only I remembered) I started calculating how this was God working. "Ok wow, that's crazy that I met him again about the same date AND in the same location, but this time I am single. Gods timing is perfect". Word to the wise, when God is working, so is the devil. About a week later I ran into him again in

86

the parking lot when I was leaving work. We had not yet talked on the phone yet, I guess he was too busy to call. Anyway, he just happened to be at the salon this day too. His side hustle of selling products gained him a big clientele at the salon that I was working at. Once we were both in the parking lot, we got the chance to talk a little more this time. We played questions and answers for a while.

Me: "How many kids do you have"?

Him: "2, how many do you have"?

Me: "2, a girl and a boy"

Him: "me too"

The surface questions continued. I was happy with the answers. Yes! One mother for both the kids! Lawd knows I didn't have time to be dealing with no drama. As we were talking he just kept looking over his shoulder. I remember getting scared and asking if there was someone after him because he was acting really jittery. The questions and conversation rolled on for about 15 minutes before parting ways. In that convo he said, "At the end of the day I am not looking for a girlfriend, I am looking for a wife". Those words right there was music to my ear. This was God right? Was God finally sending me what I wanted and deserved? That may have been my husband that I was talking to. All of these thoughts crossed my mind as I drove home that night. In the weeks passing

we talked and texted before going out. When I finally decided that
I wanted to go out with him, I did not want to go alone. I had to
call my cousin to be my wingman for the night just incase I wasn't
enjoying myself and wanted an excuse to leave. Thank God she
was available. We met him on U Street in DC to pick him up and
from there we headed to a bar. Now the story was, my cousin and I
were already out when he called me to go out, so I could go but,
she would be with me. He was cool with that and we went to some
low-key hookah bar Uptown in DC. I wasn't ready for anyone to
see me out yet. This was also why I had my cousin Britt in place to
wing it with me, that way no one could confirm that I was on a
date. For all they knew he could have been with her so it was the
perfect cover-up. We were at the bar eating, drinking, talking and
laughing. We were having a good time, until the bill came and he
reached over and said, "aye babe how much is mine"? Him asking
me that really threw me off. I did a double take. I was so annoyed
with his question that I paid for both of us. I excused myself to the
bathroom and texted Britt: "Girl come to the bathroom". When
she knocked on the door I thought it was him so I didn't say
anything. Then she started banging, I was thinking "oh this niccuh
is really crazy". She was like, "girl open the door its ME"!! I opened
the door and we were cracking up laughing. I said "GIRL we need
to drop this niccuh off!! I'm going to say we have to go pick up
your daughter". We agreed and went back to the bar to meet "El
Cheapo". We left and got in the car. I started driving and I said,
"Where we going boo"? He was like "Uhh I mean we can go to U
Street or to a club or something". I said, "Nah boo where am I

taking you? My cousin has to go pick up her baby, and I have to take her". He was like, "Oh ok you can drop me off at home". I sped through the city trying to get that boy home. We pulled up and I told him I would call him later. Once he closed the door and we pulled off I was like, "OH HELL NO!! GIRL WTF!! I cannot believe this clown asked me how much was his! UGH"! We laughed and sped off all the way to the next restaurant for more food and drinks. In fact, we laughed him out the entire night. The following week he called and texted me and I completely ignored him. Not to teach him a lesson but simply because I didn't want any parts of him. He sent me super long texts telling me how he saw a future with me and I really hurt him. I was at home reading them like "huh? Dude you don't even know me". I finally decided to respond 4 days later and told him some story about me leaving my phone at my grandmother's, I can't remember what I told him. The way that he responded was if we were in a long term relationship, it was a bit scary and a turn off. I don't like people to get too serious too soon because I feel like something about them isn't right. I prayed that I would not see him when I went to work and that prayer was answered for a few weeks. One day, he caught me slipping when I wasn't paying attention while I was eating my lunch in the salon waiting area. I looked up and he was right there! He instantly started explaining how hurt he was by my actions. I drifted off into a daydream as I heard almost nothing that he was saying. I was in my head thinking, "What in the hell is wrong with this dude"? He continued on and said, "I could go out here and get hit by a bus and you wouldn't care, you are so heartless". That's the only part I caught because I instantly came out of my daydream and thoughts. Something about him saying that kind of pierced my heart. "Heartless"? I questioned myself, "how am I being heartless"? I explained to him that wasn't the case and I was just busy. I decided that I would give him a second chance and not write him off just yet. I finally came clean as to why I was ignoring him. He had a pretty understandable defense. He said he had been in situations where women would bring a friend on a date and expect him to pay and he wasn't going for it that night. Ok, I can understand that, to some degree. On the other hand I'm like why not just pay for you and your date. Once we cleared the air we went on our second date, which I ended up having a wonderful time. He paid. No complaints. Everything was kosher. He was very charming, in the beginning. He liked to do all the random things that I loved to do. One of the first things we did was take a random trip up to Philly. He called me and asked what I was doing, and I lied and said "nothing about to drive to Philly to see my cousin, but I am afraid of driving over the Bay bridge". This was the test to see if he was my type of guy, the type to get up and go random places with me. His answer was "come on, let's go"! This was around 10:00 at night on a Saturday. Before I knew it we were driving up to Philly, well I was doing the driving, until we got to the Bay Bridge. We pulled over and switched seats and he got us across safely. I remember keeping my eyes closed and holding his hand, this was the beginning of me trusting him because that bride is one of my worst fears. We got across, and continued our quest. I remember thinking, "wow God, this is it. This is the husband you had for me". These thoughts ran through my mind as he uttered every little thing I could possibly want to hear. We had a great time while we were there. He liked to plan out random dates. That was something that I really appreciated because I had just got out a relationship where I had to beg for time. I was finally spending time with someone that wanted to spend time with me and take me out without me having to beg and plead him. When the weather broke and it was warm, we did some of my favorite romantic things. Some of those things included, going on ice cream dates on random afternoons, and taking long walks in the park to sit and watch the sun set. Initially he was just, "my friend". One day we went on a day date at the harbor and he said he had something special for me. He took me on the Ferris wheel that day. When we got off we took a long walk down by the Gaylord Hotel. We walked. We talked. We laughed. He sat me down and started to give a speech and asked me to just listen. He expressed to me how he had never met a woman like me and he saw so much in the future for us. He continued on to serenade me with his words. He actually was reading from a letter that he wrote. A man that writes letters, "oh God, this IS you, I know it is". I am a sucker for simple romantic gestures like a hand written letter. After he read the letter he said, "omg, I am so nervous. Give me a minute". I was looking at him and thinking in my head, "what the heck is going on, I KNOW he is not about to ask me about no marriage". I eliminated that thought very quickly and as soon as I was exiting the thought, I looked and he was on his knees. He continued on and said, "I know it is still early for me to ask if you would marry me". My

thoughts interrupted his words, "umm you got d@mn right it is".
He continued, "But I want to ask you would you consider marriage
with me in the future. This is not a proposal. I just want to know if
in the future will you THINK about it". Well, the thought had
already happened the day I met him. So yeah, it was ok to "think"
about it right? I already thought about it. We all kind of picture
things. So, I said "yeah, I would consider it". He got up excited like
I said "yes", first of all I said "yeah" and that was to me
"considering" the "thought". He pulled out a ring and placed it on
my finger. He said it was a "promise" ring. I "promise" I thought it
was real, until one day that thing fogged up in the middle of me
curling a client and never un-fogged. Our first summer together
was full of dates, random trips, and quality time. "Funny how time
flies when you're having fun", Janet hit that nail on the head. I was
having so much fun, I didn't realize what was going on with his
relationship with his kids. He knew my "mommy schedule", that
was not to be interrupted and he was not to be a part of my kid's
life. It was way too early for my liking. I had no idea when he
would talk to, or see his kids. I would randomly ask and his
response was that he and their mother was going through a custody
battle, so he was not able to see his children during that time. I
remember ease dropping in on a few conversations with him
talking to other family members when his kids was with them, but
it was clear that he was not able to come around them. One day I
overheard him saying, "I know they want to see me but I can't
come over there because it's in the court order". I never got
around to ask about that situation. He gave me a whole rundown

on how his "babymomma" was bitter and did not want him around the kids. At the time, it wasn't unheard of to me because I had heard this same story from my male cousins in my own family. This wasn't enough for me to write him off as a "dead-beat" dad. To me this was a typical situation of parents not coming to an agreement, and an example of how "hurt people, hurt people". Despite what Brandon and I went through, one thing we never did was hold our kids hostage from each other. My thing is, if a father wants to be involved and is not harming the child, LET THEM. There are enough fathers out here that don't take care of their children. The worst thing that you can do to your own children is to keep them from a loving parent that wants to be involved. Your kids should never be held accountable for their other parent's shortcomings in the relationship you two had. I am not saying that this was Peter's situation because I honestly believe he was lying about something with that whole situation. At the time I did believe him. It wasn't until after getting to know him and his deceitfulness that I was able to reflect back and come to my own conclusion that he was lying. Because I believed him at the time, we continued our dating schedule. Every week we were doing something; concerts, comedy shows, dinner, or whatever else that sparked our interest. I'm the type that doesn't care what we are doing, I just want to know that spending time with me is something you want to do, even if it's just sitting up watching TV. I just love time and attention, and he was giving me all of his. It may have been too early for with me just getting out of a relationship to be entering a new relationship, but that's what I was doing.

Jumping from one relationship to the next was where I messed up in my healing process. The advice that I would give any woman when going from one relationship to the next without taking time out for herself is, don't! That is a big mistake that I made on my part. Do I now regret it? No, because now I have the insight to share with someone else. In the beginning of Peter and I's relationship, Brandon and I were still living in the house together. We were both doing our own thing and sleeping in separate rooms. We had the perfect co-parenting schedule. I was in the house with the kids Sunday-Thursday and he was Thursday-Sunday. There was no messing around going on with Brandon because I was fully committed to Peter. Thursdays through Saturdays belonged to Peter and me. These were "our days". On our days I would stay at his house and live a separate life. One thing about them tables baby, they do turn. Brandon started to seriously FEEL IT. I would leave out the house and stay out and he would BLOW MY PHONE UP! I would see it, ignore it, or sometimes flat out be bold and answer it. He would ask me if I was with someone else and I would simply tell him, "I don't have to explain anything to you". This burned him up. One day he went into my sleepover bag and found candles, lingerie, sex games, and all the other stuff that I used to have for him, but this time it was for Peter. When he called me out on it, I made it clear that it was not his business. He was seeing a different "Ki" and not liking her at all. This living arrangement went on for about 4 months until Brandon realized it was over for good and it was time that he moved on. He continued to help with the bills, as a real man should when his children are there. One day he found out that Peter spent the night one night and that's when the financial help for the household ENDED. When the financial help from Brandon stopped, Peter and I had been dealing with each other for about 7 months. That took a huge financial fold on my life. I mean this was the first time in my life that I had to figure out things on my own. I wasn't mad at him, I completely understood. I am a hustler by nature so I did what I had to do to move out that summer. We had two sets of furniture so I sold half of it while trying to save the money I would need for my new apartment. I was going back and forth to court with the leasing company for the house we were renting, and Peter never once offered help. My mother moved in with me and helped me a lot with the bills. Here is a rule ladies, if a man can't help you or doesn't offer to help you when he is in a relationship with you, he is just taking up space. Money isn't everything but dag on it, it does help and a REAL man would not let you do it alone. One thing about Brandon, he always made sure I was good. The entire time of our relationship he took care of most of the bills. Now there I was in a new relationship protesting how money wasn't everything, and I would rather date the trash man that treated me like a queen verses the doctor that treated me like trash. I am not going back on my word with that, however there are layers to that belief. No man should sit back and watch a woman do it on her own without offering help. I'm going to need that trash man to go out of his way and do all he can do to help his woman. Yes in the very beginning everything was fun and romantic. It didn't take long for the layers of who Peter really was to peel off. We were already spending our one on one time together, but he wanted more. Peter did not respect my space. He would call me asking me why was I keeping his "stepchildren" from him. WEIRD!! I ignored the whole "stepchildren" part, and expressed how I had to be extra careful with my (at the time) 8 year old daughter. This was not a basketball game where her father was out and he got put in the game. She needed to heal too. Her father has always been VERY much involved in her life and now was not the time for confusion. I protected my babies as much as I could during the healing process as things were changing for them as well. Until, one day Peter robbed me of that. He called me and asked what I was doing and I told him I was at the zoo with my kids. He told me that he was going to come up there, I told him DO NOT come and I meant just that. He popped up anyway and I wanted to snap, it took everything in me not to. This man was really trying to look like we were a family. He tried to push my sons stroller and I felt so uncomfortable, I was like "I got it, thanks". He was so pushy. My uncle gave me dating advice when I first met Peter and it was, "don't pay attention to the big things a person does, pay attention to the little things in the beginning because those are the things that will become the bigger issues later". This was just the beginning to the pushy, manipulative person that he was. Not only did he rob me of my boundaries that day, but he also robbed my daughter of her comfort. He approached a stranger and asked that she take a picture of us all. I know it was just a picture, and maybe it wouldn't have felt so weird if he had not imposed on us the way that he did. My daughter looked so uncomfortable when he put his arm around her to take the picture. I was so annoyed and when I went back to look at the picture, I could see the pain, confusion and hurt all over her face. It broke my heart. THIS was why I needed the time and SPACE I requested. This man really tried to manipulate my beliefs. He tried to make me think that life was so short that nothing should have a time stamp on it. To a degree he convinced me of that but NOT when it came to my children. Especially NOT to my 8-year-old daughter that was in the process of processing what was happening to her family. "All the women I used to deal with would let me meet their kids within the first two-weeks", said Peter. "Well those women were crazy as hell because ain't no way I'm letting no man around my kids that soon" I exclaimed! Not only was it hot as hell that day at the zoo but also I was BURNING up in the inside. The combination of both degrees of heat almost sent me into an explosion. I held my composure for the sake of my kids. They had no idea that Mr. Peter was actually mommy's new boyfriend. I lied and told my daughter that he was one of my older friends son that just happened to be at the zoo that day and he needed a ride home. He wasn't too happy with that story but he went with it. He didn't have the boundaries that I had with his kids with his kids. A lot of men bring women around their kids early. I remember the day that I met his daughter. I went to pick them up. As soon as she got in the car he said ,"This is daddy's new girlfriend, Ms. Rickia". It was just straight to the point. Before anything, I am a mother and a woman, so with uncomfortable situations I would have to break things down for him. "You can't just push me off on your kids like that, kids need time to process things". Of course he didn't get that, he had no structure to his parenting style. The second time I met his daughter, he got in the car and said, "I told my daughter that we were taking her shopping down the harbor". Don't let the part of "he got in my car" go over your head. He claimed his car was in the shop when we first met, I guess that was a lie. He didn't have a car. He didn't have a license. All of our dates and meet ups required me driving my brand new car to pick him up, drop him off, take him to meet his customers, get his kids, etc. Issa "uber girlfriend"! His daughter got in the car and I said "hi". She was not as social as she was on our first encounter. As I pulled off of the parking lot, I was thinking, "She looks different from the first time I met her". I decided to opt out of any awkward conversation with baby girl in the car, so I waited. When I dropped her off I said, "That's not the same daughter that I met the last time". I wanted to sound confident, for if it were a lie, now was the time for him to be honest. He said, "I know that's my other daughter". WHAT!? Other daughter? If he has two children, one boy and one girl how is there another daughter? I was trying to figure out this equation as if I was a child and my mother was yelling at me doing my math homework like; "IF 1 PLUS 1 IS 2! WHAT IS 1 PLUS THREE"!? Then, me crying saying "5" and getting slapped upside the head. I just couldn't wrap my head around it. So I said, "you told me you had 2 kids". His lying azz said, "No I told you I had 3 kids". This turned into an argument, because where I come from people don't lie about their kids. If they have multiple kids and multiple mothers they are taking care of their kids and not hiding the facts. I was ready to do my own research, so I went on his instagram and went through ALL of his pictures as soon as he go out of my car. I saw pictures of kids but at this time I had not been around the kids long enough to tell who was who from old pictures. Since I couldn't prove any solid evidence other than him lying about the amount of kids he had, we moved passed this particular lie. He took me out to dinner and explained to me that I had "misunderstood" him and that he said that he had 3 kids. I still knew there was no way that I could misunderstand that, but whatever. The truth was out now, at least that's what I thought. He was really good with wanting to sit and talk things over dinner, another small gesture that intrigued me. I thought, "Wow, that is what men do, they want to sit over dinner and discuss things like adults". I wasn't used to that, but I liked the fact that he was willing to solve a problem versus getting mad and walking away. We picked up on the good part that we left off on and kept things moving. It was still the summer and I was living my best life. I was running the miles UP on my brand new car! I was taking him lunch everyday on my off days while my kids are at school. He was still making time for me and things were great. He was giving me the time that I was yearning for, so if it took me doing all the driving, pick-ups and drop-offs, I was with it. The days the kids were gone gave me the feeling of being 19 all over again. I was able to come and go as I pleased, hang out, and just feel like I had no responsibilities. The time that should have been spent working on my business, branding, promoting and marketing mostly went to Peter and what he had on his list of things to do. We were good. Everything was laid on the table. We had no more secrets. He was my "best-friend". I was so used to being in the house with my kids most of the time throughout Brandon and my relationship that I think I went into freedom overdrive. Not only did I spend the days that I did not have the kids with Peter but, I even started to spend the days that I had them with him. With my mother living with us she would take care of my motherly duties while I went out and lived like I didn't have any responsibilities. I needed to slow down but I did not. The voice of my mother and friends saying that I needed to finally go out and have fun validated my actions. Not only was I spending a lot of time out, I was spending a lot of money on gas, food on our now rotating dates, bills, and whatever else. I needed to slow down and get back to my kids. I wasn't fully out of mommy mode, I would still do baths, homework, cooking (when my mother didn't), cleaning and the host of other duties, BUT once those things were done I was out the door. I started giving baths and dinner sometimes before the sun went down. Later my guilt sank in when my daughter said, "We don't have mommy and daughter day anymore, when is the last time just you and I did something together"? That one comment pierced my soul. It was time to slow down that "All Summer 16" flow. I don't know about Peter but my kids and their feelings came FIRST! My daughter needed my time and attention and I changed fast to make sure of that. My schedule quickly went back to me spending time with him on the days that I did not have the kids, and I made sure that he respected that by not over stepping his boundaries this time. The signs of me being a different caliber of woman he had ever met were there. When he first came over to my house on one of the days I didn't have the kids I could tell that he was wowed. Every place that Brandon and I have had has always been nice. I did most of the decorating. The house that we had been living in looked like something out of a magazine once I purchased new furniture, painted, and made it ours. My friends call me "The Black Martha". I may not use my money to buy bags and shoes in overload, but I will invest in where I live to make sure it looks nice. I can't say what type of women that he had dealt with before but I know that they weren't like me. He was now dealing with an upgrade. A self-employed business woman, with a college degree, nice house, a good head on her shoulders, and a very promising future. Don't you know the type of woman that all the "round the way" dudes put on the top shelf like "don't mess her over, not her"? She is also the same type of woman that when a man is not ready for her, he kindly stays out of her way because she is more precious than gold and he doesn't want to tarnish that. That is the type of woman that I am. I'm convinced that LL Cool J song "Around the Way Girl" is about me every time I listen to it. "Around the way, you're like neighborhood jewel". I am that jewel! I could tell he was used to dealing with "girls from around the way" but NOT THEE "Around the way GIRL". We are not the same. The first person to tell me that I could do so much better than Peter was my very own sister. One day I took him with me to get her so that we could go out for some drinks. Before going she wanted to go to the corner store, so we made a quick stop. All of a sudden when she got back to the car from buying him a candy bar (which he asked her to get without him even reaching for any money like a real man would) she changed her mind and no longer wanted to go. I found that weird but, sometimes my sister just doesn't like people so I didn't think anything of it. Later that night, she texted me saying that she was trying to figure out where she knew him from, and realized she knew who he was once we dropped her off. She ranted on about how he was not even a man that met my standards. She told me I could do so much better and all he does is use women for his benefits. I was thinking, "She is tripping". She was talking about situations from years ago. Who I was dealing with was not who she was talking about. People change. He changed. From that point on she did not give him a chance. This created much distance between her and I. She would call me and hear him in the background and just "CLICK", hang up. It wasn't that I did not believe what she was telling me, I just did not believe that he was still the same person that he was during the time she was speaking of. My sister holds me at a high standard and I understood she was trying to protect me but I just didn't agree with her at the time. I was blinded to everything she was saying because I had not been exposed to who she said he was. When it comes to people we love and care about, and the relationships they are in, sometimes its best we just pray that God reveals the truth. Sometimes intervening can be misunderstood. The truth will always be revealed. We didn't talk or see each other as much during that time. My sister loves hard, and when she loves you, everything that you do that she may not agree with takes over her life. I would have to tell her sometimes "you just got to let people live their life, they will figure it out". Her loving hard can be confused with being judgmental if you don't understand her heart. She was only trying to help me, but her approach on helping me pushed me away. She was right though, I deserved so much better, and I didn't find that out until later. Even he knew I deserved better. One day he said, "sometimes I feel like you are just too much for me and I can't live up to your standards. So maybe I should be with someone that doesn't have as many standards". I was not willing to lower my standards and he was not willing to be done with me, so he had to step up in the areas he lacked for me not to lose interest. He did what he could and I gave him credit for that. Sometimes when you are used to certain things a man has exposed you to it's hard to go backwards. It was the little things that he wasn't used to doing that I expected from a man. I did believe he was teachable. He needed basic training on the simple things:

-Taking trash out (*The way I was raised, it is a mans job when he is around to take the trash out, period!*)

-Pumping gas (*Another thing women should not do when a man is around. A man instantly looks like he has female tendencies when he is ok with this in my book.*)

-Going into stores (*A woman should never go into a store at night by herself while a man sits in the car. You can go in for me or we can go together.*)

There are a few other things but that's just the surface. I had to school him on these things because he didn't really understand what the big deal was with a woman doing these things while a man was around. Too many of us women are out here raising grown men. Some men need to be taught certain things (and that is sometimes ok) but some things should be taught early on. I have never had these conversations in my previous relationship. The relationship that Brandon and I had was pretty old school. He paid the big bills, I paid the utilities. He walked on the side of the sidewalk closer to the cars. I hardly ever paid for gas, let alone attempting to pump it. Now granted we had a lot of issues that needed to be fixed, but I will say he knew the basics of a man's role. Peter tried to step his game up, but he wasn't able to keep up with the tone that Brandon had set before him. But, people change. All I had to do was just teach him how to treat me. But did I have the time to was the real question. Brandon and I had been together since we were 19. When we broke up I was about 30 or 31 years old. We taught each other so much. The difference was with Brandon and I being together since teenagers, we had the time to teach each other things. But at 30 years old and older, I feel like I don't have that type of time anymore. Do you really want to be playing Mrs. Fix-him-up or Mr. Fix-her-up in your 30's or older? My 20's were the years where I was trying to figure out who I was. Today I am 33 going on 34 and I am just at a place in my life where I am VERY comfortable in who I am. If I were single and a man didn't have it together by now, I just wouldn't have the time to mentor him in figuring out his life. At the time I had very MINIMAL time and patience to play "Mrs. Fix-him-up" with Peter. His time was on thin ice. Just when I thought all of his lies were on the table, the lie party was just getting started. Here we go with the foolery.

6 DEAD ENDS
SOMETIMES YOU HAVE TO CUT THINGS BACK TO GROW

One day we were on our way to dinner when Britt called and said, "You by yourself"? I said, "No". She said, "okay call me back when you are by yourself". I should have never answered the phone on my car's Bluetooth. When I ended that call Peter was so upset! He wanted me to call her back and act as if I was by myself, but my loyalty towards my cousin came first and I said, "NO". I had no idea what she wanted to tell me and I was not about to potentially put her business on the front line for him to hear. After he realized I was not about to let him ear hustle, he got even more furious as we went in the restaurant. I let "Mr. Attitude" sit by himself at the bar while I excused myself to the restroom to call Britt back. When she answered the first thing she said was, "Does he have a baby on they way"? I was completely blindsided by her question, I was like "Girl NO". She asked me was I sure, and I told her that I was almost sure he didn't have a baby on the way. She told me she was going to send me a picture and for me to call her once I got it. It seemed like forever for the picture to come through. When it came through my heart dropped to the floor. It was a collage of him, a sonogram and this pregnant girl. My mind went blank, and I told her that I would call her later. I questioned myself the entire time walking to the table "why would God put me in this happy place just to remove me"? I know we shouldn't question God, but at the time I did. My entire mood changed. Soon as I sat down he could tell that my entire attitude changed. He started acting really nervous and told me that he was ready to go. We left without eating. When we got to the car I asked him if there was anything that he thought I should know. Of course he lied and said "no". He asked me what was wrong, and I told him that I was waiting on him to tell me what he thought I should know. He insisted that there was nothing to tell me and got so mad at my response that he jumped out my car. Big mistake! I was gone off him, but not to the point that I wouldn't pull off. I left him where he was standing. Skurt!! I went home so that I could process what I was just informed. I turned my phone off for about 3 hours before turning it on to call him. To my surprise he was still in the same area that I had left him and asked me to meet him so we could talk. Once I got there he instructed me to head to his house so that we could talk about it there. He ultimately used me for a ride! When it was time to talk he still denied that there was anything that he needed to tell me. Frustrated, I snatched my phone out and pulled up the picture and said; "So you are telling me this is not your baby"? He calmly said, "no". Then he went into this long story about how he had met this girl over the summer and just found out a week ago that she was pregnant and she said the baby could be his or some other guy's. He said that he was SURE that the baby wasn't his because they never had unprotected sex. Again I am a woman and mother first. My first thought was, "I would not go out of my way posting a picture of him and my baby unless I knew that he was the father for sure". I told him I needed time to process everything because I am not the woman to come into something and say "he is not the father". I don't know, I wasn't there. This was not something that I would sweep under the rug. Again, I wasn't raised around men who didn't take care of their kids so

I dag on sure was not going to knowingly enter a relationship with a man that wasn't taking care of his. He should me his first sign of being mentally unstable. He began to yell and scream begging me not to leave him. He said "somebody going to die and I don't care about no police, no news or nothing". I didn't feel like he was directing the message to me, but he was definitely insinuating hurting someone else. I figured he was just talking out of anger, but still, some things you just don't say. I should have stopped dealing with him at this point, but I didn't. I continued the relationship operating more as if it was his baby. If he wanted to be with me he would have to be a father to his child FIRST. I encouraged him to take a DNA test once the baby was born to find out for sure. He said that he would and I pressed the issue. Months went by and during that time I did my own research. Well what do you know, I had been following the girl on instagram the whole time. Liking her cute preggo pictures and everything, not having a CLUE that this was "potentially" (let him tell it) the mother of his unborn child. God always gives us signs. It was right in my face and I didn't see it. During her pregnancy, I periodically checked her page to keep up with his lies. I was looking on her page to find out when the baby was due so that I could be able to clock him with the next lie. I remember saying, "I hope this baby is not born on my birthday". The due date was close enough to my birthday for me to make that wish. I was planning on sticking by him and I just still wanted to have my day to myself at the least. It's one thing to find out about something like this, but it's another thing to be constantly reminded on your birthday. I was informed that the baby had been born, not by him, but via social media, and yes ON MY BIRTHDAY. Guess who never mentioned it? Peter. On the way to my birthday dinner, I approached him and asked why didn't he tell me. He said it was still my day and that I should not be concerned about that because it wasn't his baby. For me to be comfortable in the relationship I needed to know for sure if the baby was his or not. He came up with tons of excuses as to why he couldn't take the test. One day he sent me a picture of something in his phone. What he didn't realize was he sent the picture with the tiny pictures of other pictures at the bottom. I zoomed in as far as I could zoom, and I saw a picture of him holding the baby he claimed wasn't his. He came up with another story. This time it was that he ran into the girl on his lunch break, and he asked her about taking the paternity test and she said she didn't want to. He said that she asked him if he wanted to hold the baby and he said, "I guess". He said she then hurried and snapped a picture of him and that she didn't understand why he needed a test. If we had a relationship and all of a sudden he dipped out and needed a paternity test, I would feel the same way. At this point in the relationship he had 3 kids and now a 4th possible, until paternity to the other baby was confirmed. We moved on yet again. Sometimes he would sit across from me and I would be looking at a picture from social media comparing her cute face to his lying face. One day I looked and said to myself, "She looks just like his other daughter. Why would he not want to own up to being the father of his child"? All of this was before I even met or thought of him. Each time that I would ask him about the baby, he had a different excuse and still denied being the father. Despite what he would say, I still periodically asked. I continued to ask him every 2 months through the reminder of our relationship. In the beginning we all look over certain behavior patterns. By now the beginning phase was phasing out. He lied about everything and I do mean everything! Even the dumbest things! He was the type to lie for no reason. He could be eating a cheeseburger and I could ask him what he was eating, and he would say a crab cake. He definitely had "liabetes" LOL. When we first met, another turn on for me was how caring he was for his mother. He took her in and let her come live with him by taking the stress of paying bills off of her. Later I found out that was a lie too and he was the one living with her. Living with his mom wasn't the issue. The issue for me was that he was trying to portray a false image. I never addressed that issue because I wanted to save him the embarrassment. The relationship was becoming more and more draining and embarrassing. When I would threaten him to leave him, he would come up with some very extreme manipulative antic. One time we were in the car arguing about something, I can't remember what it was, but he pulled another act on me. This fool got out the car and laid in the middle of the street and said he wanted to die. Mental illness is real, but manipulation is real too. There is a thin line between the two. He must have known this street because, no cars were coming. Finally, one came and I came running to pull him out of the street. Another time, he tapped a butcher knife to his throat and attempted to press is neck on the wall with it. I "saved" that day too. He had an act and lie for everything! One day one of my clients (turned friends) sat in my chair asked how everything was going with my relationship with Peter. I told her everything had been great, except for the latest situation with me finding out about the baby. I wasn't hesitant on telling her because she has become like a sister to me that I love and trust. When I told her what was going on she was shaking her head crying, and said she had saw the very same picture on instagram. She battled with coming in that day to tell me. She asked her aunt for advice and her aunt asked that she pray on it. Her prayers were answered, fast. She said she worried so much about it and me telling her was a weight lifted off her shoulders. God saved me the embarrassment of knowing before one of my clients would tell me. At that point I was wondering how many other clients knew about this but were afraid of telling me. The thought of how many others may have known was very embarrassing. Little did I know there was more embarrassment to come. I had been building a relationship with his kids as he was with mine. I was around them so much to the point that I was doing drop-offs and pick-ups without him. One day I was dropping one of his daughters off and her mom asked me if I had met his other daughter. I said, "not yet". When she said the child name I specifically remember him having a convo with this same child in the beginning of our relationship. I never forgot her name because it was so pretty. When she asked me, I had to fake like I wasn't completely thrown off. When I pulled off I called him IMMEDIATELY and asked who was this other child that his daughter's mother was speaking of. I mentioned the name of the child and he told me that his daughter's mother was full of drama, and she liked to keep things started, so that was a lie to start some drama. He said that the child she was speaking of was probably one of his daughter's cousins or friends. I was taking notes because the truth would come to light at some point. I still gave him another chance to be honest. One day I was in my room while he was sitting up in my bed and I asked him, "Be honest with me, how many kids do you have"? His answer was, "How many kids did I say I had"? Then after a long pause he said, "I have 3 kids, why do you keep asking me"? I added, "and a possible" to alert him to stop trying to dismiss the other baby situation that he needed to handle. In this conversation I felt the heaviness of an evil spirit around me. My eyes started to water and I said, "I feel like the devil is in this room", he smirked and said, "he probably is". I should have got him out of my house at that very moment, but I didn't. The signs that God was giving me were all there but I continued to look for more proof. One time I was waiting on him and I called his phone about 20 times. He said he was on the train and didn't have service. He was missing in action for about 4 hours. When he finally got with me he couldn't come up with a lie other than he was just riding the train. He went to touch my face and I said, "Why your hands smell like spiced amber or warm vanilla sugar"? He said it was from the soap in the bathroom. I knew he was lying, but I wanted to check the soap in my bathroom to confirm my thoughts. I faked like I was going to the bathroom and checked the soap. That soap was a dry! I went back and asked him why did he lie and then he said, "Oh, it must be from the hand sanitizer in the uber". Later he went to sleep and I went to check his jacket pockets. There were a few business cards from women, a few phone numbers, and receipts. Being as though a lot of his customers were woman, I tried not to jump to conclusions. Something told me to smell the jacket. The entire jacket smelled like warm vanilla sugar or spiced amber. I should have rested my case, but I needed more proof, like a fool. He was definitely a wolf in sheep's clothing. I could not believe that I was in ANOTHER toxic relationship. He and I started to have packing parties, just like Brandon and I did. But, with him there was not a lot for me to pack because I only set aside minimal room for his things. Most of the time, he refused to leave. One time I attempted to pack his things and before I knew it, he had grabbed me by my neck and threw me on the bed. He had his hands wrapped around my neck so tight that I was losing my breath. I told him to get off of me, once he let go, he took off running because I was going OFF. I should have known at that very moment that he had a history of being abusive. He had never hit me, but that one choking situation was more than enough. He could have killed me. Sometimes we minimize things and say, "oh he pushed me" or "he just choked me". It's all abuse and is unacceptable. A man should not put his hands on a woman in ANY aggressive way, PERIOD. Furthermore, no woman should stick around for that. Yes I stuck around after that incident and I should have made a smarter decision, but I did not. We continued what was now our up and down relationship. We continued to take our random trips. God forbid I plan anything with anyone else, he would be so pissed. My sister planned a trip for she and I to go to Puerto Rico, at the time I could not afford to go, so she paid for my entire trip. I would have done the same for her. As I was preparing to go on the trip, I started to notice him getting very jealous and upset. We got into a big argument about me going on the trip with my sister and he asked me to cut my sister off. Now he was "tripping" tripping. I cursed him out and told him that would NEVER HAPPEN! He said, "if my sister didn't like you and you asked me to cut her off I would with no problem". I said, "I wouldn't even ask you no dumb s#!t like that". I continued on and said, "I wouldn't cut my sister off for NO NI@@A! And for a n!@@a to even ask me some s#!t like that he is CRAZY". Once he realized that that would never ever ever happen, he got over it. While I was in PR, he claimed he stayed at the apartment, which I know he did not. I set him up to see for myself. I left certain things that I knew he would touch a certain way. I cleaned my whole apartment up before leaving. I cooked a big pot of spaghetti for him and made sure everything was in tact before I left. When I returned, there were no dishes in the sink, no soap used, no wet wash cloths, no plates or cups on the table, no spaghetti eaten, that niccuh ain't stay there. He never cleaned up after himself so I rested my case to myself. I never addressed that I knew he didn't stay there because now we were dealing with something unimaginable. I had just got word that his mother was killed and that was not the time for me to bring up any drama, so I dismissed it. I became one of his biggest support systems during that time. He had only been staying at my new apartment on the days that the kids weren't home. I was aware that our living arrangements would potentially become a little more permanent because of this unfortunate situation, so it was not in my heart to turn my back on him. I let him know that it was ok for him to stay, but my kids were not to know or have a clue that he was living there. I always kept my room door closed even when he wasn't there, this helped me with hiding the fact that he was living there when he moved in. My children would see him come over but they never knew that he stayed because the door would be closed. We would all congregate in the living room, and when they would go to bed he would go in the room. In their eyes, Mr. Peter was gone when they woke up, and Mommy was in full mommy mode with getting them ready in the mornings. I had a whole operation going. I was not ready for my kids to see a man lying up my bed that wasn't their father or my husband. During the funeral services for his mom, I was reading the obituary and to my surprise, I saw the name of the child that he claimed to be his daughters cousin AND the name of the "potential baby" listed as her grandchildren. On top of the amount of kids that he told me his siblings had and the amount of kids he said he had, there were some extras. It wasn't adding up. I went to the burial site and dismissed myself without announcement. I was furious! Once he realized I was gone he blew my phone up with calls and texts asking why did I leave. I get that this may not have been the time, but I thought me leaving to process all that was going on was the best thing for me. I expressed to him my concerns about the kids that he claimed weren't his being in the obituary. He said that was no reason to leave and that we could talk about it later. Later that day, he expressed to me that the baby's name was in there because the mother of the baby reached out to his niece lying, and saying this was his baby and she begged her to put the name in the program. I did not believe that at all. He proceeded to tell me the story of how this "cousin" of his other daughter was actually his stepdaughter from a previous relationship. He said that he helped raise this child and she has always called him "daddy" so that is why she was in the program. I never processed that response deep enough to believe it or not, at this point I was numb and almost immune to the lies. Weeks later, he finally admitted that the "cousin" turned "stepdaughter" was indeed his daughter. The extra kids, oh those were just kids that his mother looked at as her grandchildren. The average person would have never gotten this far right? I know, but this had to happen for me to get to the prize at the end of my rainbow. One day I finally I got to meet the daughter that he said was his other daughters cousin. She was a very sweet girl just like the other daughters that I had met. We ended up bonding really well when they would come over. I had so much fun with the three girls. They admired me and looked at me almost like a role model. On our first date with the daughter that I had just met, when we were alone she said; "I really like you Ms. Kiki. You really like my father?" I said, "Yes, I do". She proceeded to say, "Yeah he has a lot of kids". She named them all. All SIX of them! Not including the possible baby of the bunch. During this conversation she also mentioned the fact that her dad said he wanted to marry me. She said, "Would you marry him"? I said, "Do you think I should"? Her answer was, "NO, you have so much going on for yourself Ms. Ki, if I were you I wouldn't. He doesn't take care of his kids and he always says he is going to do stuff and never does it. My step daddy is my dad. He does everything for me". That blew me a way. This child who really liked me advised me to not deal with her father, she cared more about my well being than her liking me. When we got home the first thing I did was grab his mom's obituary. In the print I saw ALL of the names that his daughter mentioned, it was confirmed. I confirmed with him that I knew these were his kids and he burst out crying. He apologized for lying and said that he really needed some help. He had not been the best father and he finally admitted that he lied about his kids and how many "baby mommas" he had. At this point he had 6 kids, 5 "baby mommas", and then a possible new baby and new "baby momma". Because he was still mourning and I did not want to add any emotional stress, I told him that we would work through this but there were to be no more lies. I told him for him to be with me he needed to clean up the relationships with his kids AND their moms. Before I found all of this out, he was going way out his way for my kids; buying them stuff, trying to spend time with them, just taking to them, as he should have been with his own kids. But, I didn't see anything wrong with that, because I had no idea about the other kids that he had that he wasn't taking care of. I have always have stood on the grounds of, not judging another woman for something that we may know about a man she is dealing with, because you never know what that man is telling her or not telling her. While you may be looking at her as just as much as a deadbeat for dealing with a deadbeat, the reality may be that she has no clue about what he is hiding. I remember when I first met Peter, he told me that he was engaged and his fiancé left him, and went back to the father of her kids and married him. He said that he was taking care of her, paying her bills and she just left him for no specific reason. I actually believed him and marked up his points of being a stand up guy. Never would I have imagined that the story he told me would be part of my story of me leaving him. He is probably is somewhere right now lying on me too. LOL. I'm sure he is somewhere at this very moment with his current victim lying, and telling her how he took care of me, how we planned to get married, how he treated me so good, and I just up and left him for my "baby daddy" and married him. HA! We went from spending most of our time together to him not only being an absent parent, but also an absent boyfriend. I started to spend a lot of time by myself. At first I was upset about it, but the time gave me the time that I should have taken in the first place. His mask was fully off. I started to see more of his manipulating and controlling ways. If I were unable to do something for him he would get so upset. Everything was on his time. If I had a business meeting, he would want me to be late for my meeting so that I could drop him off to where he needed to be. I started to feel like I was in the twilight zone. I was going through worst things with him that I had ever been through with Brandon. He always compared his lies, deceit, and disrespect to Brandon. Sometimes, we date new people and tell them everything that someone in the past did to hurt us, in hopes that they wouldn't do the same things, and they end up doing the exact same things, if not worst. A good man is going to make sure that he doesn't put you through the same thing. A manipulator will do some of the very same things and expect you to be okay with it, because you dealt with it before. He got comfortable with calling me b!tches when he would get mad. His excuse would be, "Brandon disrespected you for years and said worst things". He was trying to manipulate me by using my past against me to excuse himself. I found myself getting physical again. One time I got so mad it was like a scene out of a movie. I can't recall the name of movie, but maybe you can once I tell my experience. Our phones used to stay on the nightstand at night. I started to realize he was moving very different. Ok, now I was about to play chess. He went from putting his phone on the nightstand at night, to flat out hiding it. I pay attention to everything. As I said before, he was not the neatest person on earth. He would use things and not put them back, eat and not wash dishes, leave clothes on the bathroom floor, and a host of other things that I was left to clean up after. Every night he would leave his clothes on the floor by the bed. One morning I woke up and the pants that would have been on the floor were nicely folded in the drawer. Aww look at "Mr. Clean" trying to clean up his LIES. As he laid there asleep, I went in the jeans and found his phone tucked in the pocket. I had the password and I was going to see what he was hiding. I get it, some women would say, "I don't check phones, that's insecure" blah, blah, blah. Eric had called him twice at 4 a.m. Now I am going to be honest. I am not going to check a phone unless a man gives me reason to believe that I need to protect myself. I get it all things come to light, but I didn't have time for my life to be at risk during the process. The sooner I found out the better. I went in his phone and either he was gay or Eric was a woman. I knew it was a woman. I was already hip. I would store guy's numbers under female's names when I was being sneaky when dealing with Brandon. I wanted to see what he and "Eric" were talking about. I saw them having conversations of what they ate for the day, him telling her to meet him where I just dropped him off at, him telling her he loves her, and the list went on. The part in the text that sent me over was when he said, "I'm out here hustling so that we can get this apartment". I was boil-LING! I had a pep talk with myself, you know like the memes on instagram where the frog is in the mirror? On one side he has a hood on and the other he doesn't? That was me talking to myself:

The rational me: "Go in there and be calm and ask him to explain".

The irrational me: "Naw go in there and beat his a$$ sis! He got us effed up"!

I went with the irrational me. All I remember is going into my bedroom and seeing him sleeping peacefully. I yelled, "WHAT THE F#$K is going on"? I had the phone up to his nose at this point, so him reading it at a cross-eyed view was probably impossible. When he finally realized what was going on, I had a belt in my hand and he was doing the "No-No-No" shake. If the niccuh would have added a foot step he could have been in a Kid and Play video. Before he was able to explain, I simply beat the breaks off of him. No mercy. I didn't care. I beat his a$$ from my bedroom, to the bathroom, and to the living room. The only thing that was missing from that movie clip that I can't think of was some baby oil. Thank God because that oil would have probably been my first class ticket to jail. It's something about us D.C. girls that in certain situations we have to give you the: "I'm not even from around here" speech. This is how we let a person know that we ain't the one to play with. Well that day, he got that "I'm not from around here" work. At that point, I felt like the type of structured life that I lived of being a mom, business owner, church going girl, woman of class, etc., had him mistaking me for maybe some type of sucker. I'm sure his opinion of that changed that day. He threatened to get some girls to beat me up and my response was, "make sure when you send them, you send at least 10 of them b!shes"! I am replaying that whole situation in my head and saying what I should have added. I should have said, "And while you are getting them 10, ask them for $10 a piece and get your free loading a$$ a piece of car"! LMAO! Peter came up with a lie of how this girl was his sister's best friend and he was trying to help her get back on her feet. Please don't question how I was so gullible, I have no answer for that. Here I go being the "lingering" friend, giving Peter and his lies chance after chance before chucking up the deuces. His lies were over exerting me. It was becoming a job for me to keep up with the lies he told. Pay attention to nosey men as well. This man was so nosey. If I was on a phone and he was in the living room, he would put the TV on mute to tune in to my conversation. I would pause and say, "Umm you can turn the TV back on"? If he could not get in on my conversation, it would make him so mad. Watch for people like this, especially if they are known to tell lies. Many times they are so afraid of their lies being exposed, that they will try to tap into everything to make sure their mess doesn't get out. I am a dreamer so things come to me in my dreams. I remember dreaming that I caught him texting someone and saying, "I love you" in the text. When I woke up there he was sleep with his phone on his lap. I gently tapped it to see what was on the screen and there it was, "I love you, goodnight". When I approached him about it he had a follow up lie on hand. If you haven't yet written me off as the fool, don't. By now, I think I was wearing a new ring that he gave. This time it was an "engagement ring". I would mainly wear it around him and I always took it off when I knew that I would see Brandon. He asked me why I didn't post it on instagram and say I was "engaged", I told him that I didn't want people in my business. Truth is, with all the foolery going on I was not about to publically embarrass myself. I was disappointed in myself with my decision making. I remember driving one day and at a stoplight someone ran up to my car and scared the mess out of me. It was Brandon. I thought I was being robbed so I panicked while covering my chest, and that's when he saw the ring on my finger. Of all people I was trying to hide it from him the most! He asked was I engaged and I simply said, "It's just a ring", because to me that was all it was. I could see the hurt in his eyes. I drove off feeling so many mixed emotions, stupidity and guilt were my top two. Peter continued to be comfortable with not spending as much time with me; ignoring my calls, only texting me back, and lying per usual. This gave the phone calls from Brandon time for me to entertain. His calls never stopped during the entire time I dated Peter. The texts of how he wanted his family back together would slow down, but then they would pick up. In the beginning, when Peter and I got together, I would get random flower deliveries thinking he was thinking of me, nope wasn't him. It was always Brandon. Now that I was alone most of the time when the kids weren't home, the door was left open for me to be entertained by Brandon. I started catching myself on the phone with him for long periods of time entertaining him. At the time I didn't feel like I was entertaining him but so much, because it was only him that was engaging in conversations about us getting back together. The role that I played was simply listening. I started hanging out by myself and he would call. We would talk the entire time that I was out. I would give him all the updates on my business and he was always so amped to hear about what I was doing. Peter was never too thrilled about my business ventures. One night Brandon's cousin that we call "Cuzzo" called me and we talked for about an hour. He went into how he didn't know Peter, but wanted to know what was it about him that had me so involved. I could not even answer the question. We did a compare and contrast. I could not even compare Brandon and I, to Peter and I. Brandon and I had our ups and downs, but what we built together and how we leveled up together could never compare to this sinking ship that I was now in. On that phone conversation, I remember telling Cuzzo that Brandon being my cheerleader was something I was missing. I no longer had a cheerleader in my corner. My eyes instantly watered when we were on the phone. When I got off the phone I cried so hard. I was missing my biggest fan. Brandon has always encouraged me and supported me in my business decisions. There I was dealing with someone that was completely getting in the way of my dreams. I needed a cheerleader. At this time my uncle gave me the opportunity to take over the salon in the back of his barbershop. Peter was not the least bit excited for me but he was excited for himself. I found out he was telling people that it was his business and I was in the back of the shop with him. He never once said congratulations or seemed happy about my new opportunities. At one point I was making wigs for company and my first check for working one day was $1800. Peter was telling me how good that was. I was excited and he went with me to pick up my money. Do you know that this niccuh had the nerve to ask me for $200? Oh nah son, I'm not doing that. It wasn't the fact that he needed the money, it was the fact that he wanted leach off my earnings. He was becoming more and more of my son. I was tired of doing all of cooking and cleaning, sending cash apps everyday to cover his ubers, having to beg for my money back, paying more in bills than he was, just tired of the weight of him on my shoulders! I could not even be myself around him. It wasn't like how it was when I was with Brandon, at least with Brandon I could be myself at all times. Brandon and I played all of the time. Our house was known for pranks. The first time I tried to prank Peter, we almost got into a fight. He was too serious. I was used to laughing all day everyday. I love to laugh. He had specific days set aside to laugh, those days were on Thursdays when he would go to the comedy clubs. It is one thing to be in a relationship and go through ups and downs, but it's an entire different situation to be in something and going through pure hell not being able to be yourself. I can not even say I lost myself in this relationship, I never bought my whole self into it. It was a different type of lost I was experiencing. He was robbing me of my peace so, he needed to go. I prayed that God would help me and show me the way to get him out my life. God answers, doesn't he? Yes he does. One day I was working and my girlfriend Amy, texted me saying "we need to talk". I was scared to know about what. God was sending me the confirmation that I needed. Amy and I talked on the phone for about 40 minutes. She started the conversation by saying, "Hey I know I don't know Peter and I have nothing bad to say about him. But yesterday when you and I talked on the phone and we hung up the Holy Spirit was on me so heavy. We talk all the time and I always feel good when we get off the phone, but this time it was different. I couldn't sleep or shake the feeling of worry or concern for you off of me. I was trying to figure out what was so different this time in our conversation than the times from before, and what I realized is it was him on the phone. I cried last night thinking about you. I am really scared of something happening to you. DO NOT have sex with this man. Leave him alone! Something is not right about him. He is hiding something. He is NOT the man that God wants you to marry! I asked my girlfriend if I should tell you and she said "no" and that I should just mind my business. But, I love and care about you so much I don't want to not say something and something bad happens, and I could have helped by telling you how I felt. I honestly think that Brandon is a better husband for you. I just don't want to end up going to your funeral and your kids and Brandon are standing over you crying, from something that happened to you because of Peter. God has so much for you, but you are not going to be able to see your full potential and get what he has for you as long as you are with Peter. God has so much planned for your business and Peter is blocking all your blessings". The conversation went on for much longer but that was the just of it. Now let me tell you why we all need friends like Amy. Amy is old enough to be my mother but she and I share a sister relationship. Amy is that friend that I can call about a situation and baby she is going to PRAY over my life. I trust her with making decisions on my life. She is my God sent friend. She is my friend that God sends messages through to relay to me. With these words coming through the mouth of Amy, by way of God, it was NOT to be ignored!! I had been asking God for signs and THIS WAS IT! This conversation was my CONFIRMATION! It was time for me to cut these dead ends in order for me to truly grow into who God had destined for me to be. When I say I did not WASTE ANY time cutting those dead ends after the conversation with Amy, that is an understatement. I was already headed to meet Peter for dinner and my decision-making did not have much of a delay. I needed to move quickly and swiftly. I expressed to him that I was not pleased with the relationship. We were at a restaurant sitting at a booth and on the wall of the booth was a mirror. Peter spent most of his time responding to me looking at himself in that mirror. His response to my concerns of him not being the man for me was, "okay well you know what I am a handsome man and there are plenty of desperate women out here that would love to be with me". CHECK PLEASE!! That was my cue. Key word "desperate" women, I am far from desperate. Even he saw me as putting up with his actions as desperate. That was the day I was completely done with Peter. He didn't know yet but, he was about to find out at a fast rate. It was time that I pulled the rug right from under his feet. I pulled that sucker like I was Aladdin on my way to see the magic Genie. "Gimme MY RUG back"! I am saying that using my Yvette voice from baby boy when she said, "Gimme my shake". I had no peace again and dealing with him and all his drama triggered my anxiety to levels I couldn't ever imagine.

7 RINSE
GOD REMOVE THE SPIRIT OF ANXIETY

The anxiety continued over the years on and off through my life. Sometimes it would randomly come and I would feel crazy, short of breath, scared for no reason, panicky, all these feelings that I could never put into words. My first serious attack was when I was working in a hair salon. I had so many clients waiting on me that I became overwhelmed. My heart started racing, hands started shaking, I was sweating and I couldn't catch my breath. The anxiety hit me out of nowhere. I stood there shaking and saying, "I don't know why I am so anxious". This was the first attack that led me to the hospital via ambulance. My doctor put me on medication to control it, but my mind was telling me that the medication was making it worst. Things that would trigger my anxiety were excitement, worrying, stress, lack of sleep, and overthinking. When I was with Brandon and we had arguments, I would go to sleep, and wake up having an anxiety attack. It was something that I could not describe to others because people did not understand it, and that made me feel so alone. I am already a person that stays to myself so not having someone that could relate to what I was experiencing made me feel depressed. Anxiety is scary. Everyday I would feel like something was going to happen to me. Anxiety feels like a slow death. When my daughter was 6, I remember having a conversation with her. I said, "If something were to ever happen to mommy, the first thing I need you to do is DO NOT PANIC, pick up the phone and call 911". From there I gave her a list of others to call. I wrote a note on the refrigerator with directions of what I told her and a list of important numbers, and always reminded her that it was there. I hated to put such a big responsibility on her so young, but I needed to. At the time it was always me, her and my son who was a new born. Brandon was too busy out with his friends and hardly home, so I couldn't depend on him being there or being able to reach him in the event of an emergency. Being a mom helped me push through my anxiety attacks. "I CAN'T LET THEM DOWN, THEY NEED ME", I always told myself this. My kids didn't ever see me have an attack. I would be driving them to school in the middle of an attack and I would just pray until it was over. I didn't want the spirit of anxiety to cast over my kids, so I hid it from them very well. My kids have been the cores of my strength through most of what I have dealt with since having them. It is very important to protect your space and your inner peace. I learned that this was the key to my healing from anxiety. The levels of anxiety that I experienced when dealing with Peter were beyond what I could ever describe. I felt CRAZY!! When I got the new business opportunity to open my salon in the back of my uncles barber shop, I could not focus. I had this grand opportunity in front of me but I couldn't move because my anxiety held me hostage. It was like I was trying to move but my feet got stuck in wet cement and dried. I was stuck! My anxiety was in full effect, everyday and I felt so lifeless. Many times I would have these attacks in the middle of working on a client. I would excuse myself, go in the back of the salon and cry and pray!!! I prayed so much in the salon that back office became my prayer room. "God I need you! Remove this spirit of anxiety away from me. Take it away. Take it away. Take it away. TAKE IT AWAY! God I NEED YOU!! Help me to feel like myself again and feel balanced. I just want to feel normal and be able to enjoy life. God you know what I stand in the need of. God I need you! I thank you in advance for removing this evil spirit away from me", this became my daily prayer. My anxiety taught me how to become a master at praying. I knew that the enemy wanted what I had, but I also knew that God would put a stop to all that the enemy had planned, if I just turned to him in prayer and trusted him during the process. The anxiety attacks continued on a regular basis and so did my praying. Anxiety is real ya'll. It is nothing to laugh or joke about, unless you are the person dealing with it. Sometimes I would find funny memes on instagram that made me laugh at myself. It is one of them things where it wasn't funny when it was happening, but sometimes you can push yourself to laugh with some humor. One of my most recent attacks that I was able to make humor of, stemmed from me doing a self-check breast exam. I make sure I check monthly while I am in the shower standing. This particular time, I checked them in the shower and everything was fine. For whatever reason, I wanted to check them some more. I laid on the bed and checked again. Everything felt fine. I took it a step further once my anxiety kicked in. I went on YouTube and saw different women checking theirs in various ways. I had always done circular motions but when I saw one lady doing up and down motions, I decided to try that way. Everything still felt fine, until I found the lady with the lotion. There was one lady that was checking her breast with lotion, she said that you could feel them better when using lotion. I checked using the lotion, it was definitely a different feel. With the lotion I felt everything, but I figured since every breast tissue felt similar I was doing it right. UN-TIL....I started going up and down and felt something that I thought felt un-normal. I jumped my naked butt up and started to scream at the top of my lungs. I was home alone. I had to coach myself through the anxiety attack that I had triggered. "Today is amazing! You are fine! You are healthy! Everything is normal"! I repeated these affirmations to myself with each circular and downward motion. Then, I felt it again, and screamed again! I was off of work this day, so I was in no rush to get anywhere. I continued to do the breast exam again. And again. And again. "Girl you are really crazy, something is wrong with you", I affirmed to my self out loud. I spent over 7 HOURS checking my breast that day. I did not get not one thing accomplished. I even dozed off around lunchtime in the middle of my exam, woke back up and continued to feel up on my breast. Before I knew it, it was getting dark and it was almost time to pick up the kids from aftercare. If you aren't laughing by now, just wait. This is just the beginning. When I got the kids home from school, I got them situated with dinner, baths, and our evening routine. SOON as they were in the bed, I took my clothes off and got BACK in the bed to continue some more. We are in the present, so my now husband, Brandon came home and said, "You aight, you were checking your breast when I left, why are you checking them again"? I brushed it off so he didn't think I was tripping and I said; "Oh, no everything is fine. I was just double checking". I stopped checking, that is until he went to sleep. I picked the lotion back up and continued to rub where I left off. Laughing yet? Yes? You aren't at the peak of your laugh, just wait. No? It's coming, no worries. The NEXT morning, I repeated the entire breast exam movement. I got back in the shower, checked there. Got back in the bed, checked there. Got back on YouTube, checked in more newfound ways. Brandon caught me again and said, "Ki, what are you doing? You got me worried, you sure you are ok? Why don't you make a doctor's appointment"? I reassured him, while trying to convince myself, that I was "fine", again. Then I asked him to feel to see if he had felt anything weird. I placed his hand under mine and proceeded to rub both our hands on the area that concerned me. He was like, "I don't feel anything", that made me exhale some relief. Soon as I exhaled, he said "Ohhhh!! Ohhhh! Yeah! I feel it!! You talking about that right there"? OMG! I started to lose my mind at that point. He jumped up and put his hands on his head saying, "Call your doctor! Let's go NOW! Man Ki, if something is wrong with you I am going to be crushed. If something happens to you I don't know what I am going to do. We need you! OMG!! I'm stressed out." Nothing that he said comforted me. He was panicking and so was I. I called my doctor and was able to get an appointment for the next morning before I had to go back to work. After I made my appointment, I got BACK in the bed and continued. He said, "Why are you still checking? Just wait to see the doctor tomorrow". I didn't listened. I continued. He went downstairs for a couple of hours and when he came back, I was no longer in our bed checking my breast. I was IN MY DAUGHTER'S BED CHECKING MY BREAST! I really thought that switching beds would make my breast feel different. This is anxiety yall, it is a mental illness! Once I got out of her bed, I went to go check in my son's room on the floor. LMAO!! My doctor's appointment could not come fast enough. I finally got tired of checking and went to sleep that night without checking. I had become addicted to checking my breast. The next morning, I called my mother-in-law and told her everything that I just told ya'll. She got really quiet on the other end of the phone for about one minute. That one-minute was enough for me to confirm that she was worried as well about my breast. After a minute of silence, she said "Ok, this is a joke, right"? I'm still thinking she is just as concerned about my health as I was. I was crying (she didn't know) and I said, "No, it is not a joke." She startled me when she started to burst out laughing. When she realized that I wasn't laughing and I was serious, she became really concerned. Not concerned about my breast, but very concerned about my mental health. LOL. She suggested that I see a psychiatrist after I saw the doctor. When I hung up the phone with her, I kept thinking to myself that I must be crazy. Anxiety will do that to you, it will have you thinking that you are loosing your mind. When I got to my doctor, I explained everything that had transpired the days before. She really tried her best to remain professional, but she could no longer hold her laugh in when I got to the part about me being in my daughter's bed. After she finished crying laughing, she said "girl let me check out these breast so that I can get you out of here". When she lifted my shirt, she said, "OMG, they are so red"! They were red from me rubbing them! LMAO. You could even see my handprints on them, that's how much I had rubbed them. She could not stop laughing. She felt around and said, "girl these breast are perfectly fine, you are good". She prescribed me to stay off of YouTube because the people in the videos that I was watching were not doctors. As she was attempting to show me exactly how I should be checking and what I should be checking for, she asked my husband to come over so that she could show him as well. Before I knew it, she was checking my right breast, and he was checking my left breast. LMAO!!! I just laid there as they talked over me explaining how a proper breast exam should go. It is important to stay on top of your doctor's appointments and check them boobies, but please without lotion. Anxiety has its pros, I guess, because I go to the doctor for literally everything. For a long time I thought that it was just me suffering from this mental illness. Initially, I only found people that I could relate to in Google forums, never anywhere else. One day, I let the cat out the bag when I posted about my battles with anxiety on instagram, the post read: "My name is Rickia and I struggle with anxiety". To my surprise, I was not the only one in my world that was suffering from the very same thing. I got so many texts, messages, and support from people that were battling the same thing. This is the day that I stopped feeling so alone. I felt connected to others that were able to relate to what I was experiencing. I later found out that prayer was the best medicine for my anxiety. I had to be very strategic with my prayers. I may not be the most religious person on earth, however I am very spiritual and I have a super close relationship with God today. Alexa, play "I almost let go". It was God that kept me through it all. Getting certain toxic people out of my life would also be a major key to my healing as well. I chose me over everyone. It was time that I stop trying to save others and put my mask on and save myself. The first step to your journey of healing from anxiety is to identify your triggers. Find out what is the common denominator in your attacks. For me, I realized that my attacks were triggered from stress, and that included good and bad stress. If I was very excited about something, my anxiety would come jumping on me from the front, like a friend that was happy to see me. If I was upset about something, that same girlfriend named Anxiety would jump on my back and try to knock me down. Many of my attacks were also triggered from the lack of sleep. I would try to go to sleep some nights, then have an attack while I was trying to go to sleep. The attacks would get worst because I was then afraid of going to sleep and not waking up. At one point, I had so much going on in my head that I could not shut my thinking off to sleep at night. To get more rest, I would listen to sounds of water, nature, or even adult bedtime stories. There is an app that is called "Calm" and today, I still listen to the nature sounds and bedtime stories. You would be amazed at how this can help keep you calm. I use this same app to help my kids sleep at night as well. It is so funny how kids are so impressionable. Sometimes, when I go in my daughter's room to check on her, I find her phone right beside her and I can hear the therapeutic sounds of heavy rain as she sleeps so peacefully. My children do not have TVs in their rooms and I plan to keep it that way, because I do not want them being pacified by the TV to sleep at night. I used to sleep with the TV on in my room, but I have learned that my body gets the proper rest it needs with the TV off. In return, this soothes my anxiety because I feel well rested. I thank God that today I have been delivered from the spirit of anxiety. On December 10, 2018 God delivered me. I was sitting in the car praying that God would heal me in a way that only he could. I sat in the car in front of Wal-Mart and prayed before I went in.

When I would go in stores with a lot of people I would immediately feel weird, I felt anxious and the urge to hurry out. Crowded places triggered my anxiety as well. It was almost like the store was closing in on me. The thought of this happening again before I went into Wal-Mart is what resulted me to pray. I was praying all along, but after this prayer, I changed my whole approach. Before this day I was dropping sage all around the house, buying spiritual incense, lighting cleansing candles, and a host of other things. I was praying, but I was also practicing the "law of attraction" a lot. I watched the movie "The Secret" on a daily basis. I was more so going off of what they were saying; "the power of life and death is in the tongue", "your thoughts become your reality", etc. All of these things I found out to be true, but the main source of it all was having faith and praying to God. I was not giving God all the credit that he deserved. This day, I was ready to change my approach. I sat in the car and closed my eyes and asked God to clear me from anything that caused me pain. When I closed my eyes, I remained silent, and God started to talk to me in a way that I KNEW it was him. He told me that it was too loud around me, and for me to be able to position myself where I could hear him, I needed silence. He told me that he had something really big for me that would amaze me. I had my hands folded in my lap and I was there STUCK. I could not move, I could not open my mouth, all I could do is pray and listen. I started thanking him in advance (in my head) for all that he was going to do for me. The entire time that I was praying there was a ticking sound in the car and I never found out where the sound was coming from. When I was saying thank you in my head, he told me I needed to say it out loud to be able to become loosened. The more I said thank you, the more the ticking slowed down. Soon as I said THANK YOU GOD loud in my car, the ticking went "BAM" and it stopped. My body unlocked and when I got out of the car I felt different. In that moment, I kept seeing the word spiritual baptism, I have never even heard of that before. God was renewing and restoring me and it did not require me being physically baptized again. That was the last time that I experienced an anxiety attack. I experienced so much that triggered my anxiety. I hated that I even had to go through those experiences, but I now see why I had to. My pain would eventually help heal someone else. Be careful what you pray for and be very specific. I have been praying that God positions me to be able to help others. What a blessing in disguise, my pain led me to help heal myself and others. I wish my testimony could have skipped over a lot of things that I had to go through but it was very much required for my testimony. Everyday I thank God, I just can't thank him enough. It feels so good to wake up everyday and sleep at night without the spirit of anxiety. There is so much power in prayer and many times people underestimate that power. God is real, God is amazing, and he will bring you out of your darkest storms. Just go to him in prayer. I had to move things around and do so quickly before God completely healed me. I had to do a new life cleanse from all things toxic first. First toxic thing to go before my healing was Peter.

8 NEW GROWTH
ALL THINGS ARE WORKING FOR MY GOOD

Once I had that conversation with Amy, I was very serious about ending things with Peter. I was ready to listen to God and do what he asked of me. I strategically played things out. Peter's things were still there at my apartment, but he wasn't there everyday. I played him close enough for him to not act crazy and try to harm me, while I planned how I was going to get him out my house. I wasn't too sure what he was capable of because of his bipolar behavior. Since there were times before where he would threaten to harm himself or me, I had to be very strategic. I started to spend a lot of time by myself. During the alone time that I gained, I was able to pray, read and meditate. I needed to put God back in my life. He was always there but I was tuning out his voice and missing out on way too much that I needed to hear from him. I got back to my happy place. I woke up happy and went to bed happy. The anxiety continued, but it slowed down a lot when he wasn't around. I emotionally detached myself from Peter. I was just strategizing on how to completely detach myself from him. I started to go to church more consistently on Sundays before getting the kids. I grew up in the church and still attended as an adult. For a long time I stopped going, until I found a church that I felt was a better fit for me. I was turned off from "church hurt" from some of the people in my home church. When I was pregnant with my son, I went to church to tell my family as my grandfather had that Thanksgiving. I thought I would get the same acceptance as I did when my grandfather had my back, but I did not. I was on baby number 2 and still not married, so I could see why their reaction wasn't so grand, but it still hurt. Some reactions were "Congratulations", but more in a tone like "I guess?". One reaction sent me running away from the church and pretty much whoever I knew that was attached to it. I was told, "don't have no more, I forgave you for the first one". Those words pierced my heart and I managed to hold back my tears until I got in the car. I was a grown woman going on 30 years old and did not speak up for myself and say how I felt. Because my sister and I were always looked at as the babies of the family, we haven't always been recognized or respected as adults. Sometimes we get asked questions and interrogated about things that they would not ever think to impose on any other adult in the family. After that incident, I secluded myself from my family. I spent family and holiday time with Brandon's family and my father's side of the family. Church hurt, hurts a little different. You think it should be a judge free zone, but some of those people judge you more than anyone else. I started to avoid my home church because I wanted to avoid the game of questions. "When are you getting married"?, was one of the most avoided questions of my life, second to "where is your mother"? I was ready to be more consistent with church, but not at that church. I eventually got past that incident, but I still didn't feel but so comfortable there after that. During our breakup, Brandon was making sure that the kids went to church every Sunday. I was waiting on my next sign from God. I stopped going to church with Peter and started going by myself. One Sunday I went praying for the word to have my name on it. As the service began the usher approached me and said, "Would you mind moving down? We have 4 people that need to sit right here". I moved down and as I looked up to see the group of 4 people that were all together walk towards the seats, I realized 3 of the 4 people were my 2 children and Brandon. WHAT in the WORLD! Out of all the churches, out of all the seats in THIS church, out of all the TIMES at this church, and out of ALL the Sundays; how did we end up at this church, at this time and on the same row? Now granted, I put him on to the church and we were going sometimes when we were together, but this was still very random. I wasn't going every Sunday like he and the kids, and when I did go I made sure it was not the times that they went. But, EVEN still, what were the chances of them sitting right next to me out of all the seats and rooms in that church? To top it off they were very late! Usually there are other rooms to accommodate late visitors because the main sanctuary fills up fast. Okay, God you did this! The kids sat between Brandon and I so it could easily appear that we were together. We didn't speak much during service. Not out loud anyway. Our body language spoke. I know Brandon so well that I could repeat his thoughts. This day I had open toe shoes on, "yay" me for having the fresh pedi that day. I knew that his obsession with my feet would soon sink in, so I positioned my feet at the perfect angle for him to view on the sneak tip. I caught him out the corner of my eye looking. I thought to myself "yeah I know" with an imaginary smirk on my face. After service, we made arrangements of what time he would drop the kids off later and we parted ways. When he came to drop them off to me, he kept complimenting me on how good I looked at church and how he couldn't stop looking at my feet. He confirmed what I already knew. He yet again expressed to me how he just wanted his family back. I just brushed him off. The rest of that day it was hard to shake the coincidence of our encounter at church. I picked up the phone and called everyone!! "Guess who I saw at church today"!? Everyone was shocked, they thought it was a huge coincidence just like I thought. All of this time I was not thinking about Brandon. When I did think about him it was more in reference to the kids. Now all of a sudden I was having random dreams of us getting married. I knew it was no way possible that was going to happen. We were both evolving into better people and great parents. Both of us had so many great things happening in our lives, the weird part was not sharing these milestones with each other. We started to talk even more. He drilled in my head that he wanted his family back and to marry me every chance he got. For the first time in forever, I was actually picturing it. But, no, this isn't happening. He had his chance over and over again and I gave him over a decade to get himself together and he did not. Although, I may have been moving on from Peter, I was not going back to Brandon. That was my plan, but my plan and God's plan was much different. He would call me and tell me his personal business a lot and always mentioned the fact that he has yet to meet someone like me. He admitted that I was the best woman for him and he was so upset with himself for us not being together. He asked me out on lunch dates, he even invited me to go with him out of town and out the country on several occasions. One time he was in Miami and called me, "Ki, come down here! I will buy your ticket right now and fly you down here. You don't have to worry about spending any money. Lets just do a short vacation and relax". As much as I needed a break from everything, I declined his offer. This was something that Peter never did, I went to Miami with him one time and we split the cost of just about everything. I was not used to that at all. With Brandon, all I needed to do was take off of work and show up. I didn't need a wallet with him. As much as I declined his offers to take me on vacation and out various places, the thoughts of being with him were crossing my mind. One day, he came to the salon to drop the kids off, and he came to tickle me, and in the midst of him tickling me, he kissed me on the cheek. This was nothing out the norm, he had tried to kiss me on several occasions, this was just the kiss that landed. We were both on the floor while he was tickling me and the kids came running to jump on us. It was pure joy on their faces. Everyone in the salon faces lit up, as if this was potentially the start to our new beginning. He then asked me to walk with him outside, and surprisingly, I did. This was the first time that I gave him some real attention since I had been dealing with Peter. He asked me to go out to eat with him that day, I said "I will think about it". He was shocked, and so was I. I did not expect to even entertain that idea, but I did. I told him that I would call him later and let him know. He kept saying, "You are not going to call". I said, "I will". It was like it was over 12 years ago when we had just met at the tender age of 19. Later that night, after taking the kids to a party, I called him. He asked me where I wanted to go and I kept saying it didn't matter. We decided to order carry-out, and that I would come over his house with the kids since I was still in my costume from the kid's costume party. The whole drive to his house was surreal. I felt like it was not me driving. It was as if the car drove itself there. When I got there, I sat in front of his house and just looked. I thought to myself, "Wow, he really got himself together and got a house". During the 2-year break, he managed to get his credit together and buy his first house. I was so proud of him. To top it off, he bought the house that I dreamed would be our first house, and IN the area that I told him I wanted to live. When I went in the house, I kept saying, "wow Brandon, I am so proud of you, you did that". I was happy that the kids had two nice homes to come home to. He gave me a tour of the house and I enjoyed every moment. The kids were sleep, so we put them in the bed. We went down to the kitchen and talked and ate. It was like I was some alien, he just kept looking at me in disbelief. I said, "helloo.. why are you looking at me like that"? He said, "Honestly Ki, I can't believe that you are here". I

6

said, "well, it's me, I am here". For the first time since we first met, I found myself being nervous around him, omg, I like him. I like him, again. I have always loved him. Even when we weren't together, but with all the pain he caused me, I stopped liking him. They say "you like someone because, but you love someone in spite". As many times that he hurt me and as much pain as he caused me, I still loved him. My love for him has always been unconditional. But, I stopped liking him for them very same reasons. We sat on the couch and reminisced for hours. Soon, I felt myself dozing off. If you know me, you know I will fall asleep ANYWHERE and at ANYTIME. I woke up to him waking me up and telling me to get up. I was thinking, "I know he is not putting me out". He said "Ki, it's getting late and it's raining really hard. I think you should stay here. You can sleep with the kids, I won't bother you". I forgot to mention the fact that Brandon and I had not known where each other lived the entire time. When we met up to swap out the kids it was always at another relatives house, or a public place. Come to find out, we only lived about 7 minutes from each other. The only reason that he did not know where I lived was because I did not want him popping up at my house when Peter was there. His reason for not telling me where he lived was simply because he was being petty. I kept insisting that I go home because I should not be spending the night. He convinced me to stay. I went upstairs and got in the bed with our daughter. I dozed off and was in the middle of a good sleep until I woke up to the flashlight of his phone in my face. Not the light from the phone, the actual flashlight!! He was starring at me sleep. I'm not sure how long he was there before deciding to shine some light on the situation, which was, me. He pulled my hand and asked me to come in the room with him, I declined, and I dozed off again. I woke up again to hearing him talking and crying. I take that back, he wasn't talking, he was praying. I was able to hear a little of what he was saying over the crying, "God thank you so much for bringing her back. Thank you so much God. GOD THANK YOU". My eyes started to water. Soon after, he came in the room again to get me and this time, I went. I got in the bed with him and laid with him, I kept a good amount of distance though. He would not stop talking about how he could not believe I was there. There wasn't too much conversation. Before I knew it, we were spooned together as one. When I woke up in the morning I was thinking, "what in the h3ll"?! When I got up, I immediately jumped into my motherly routine, I started to clean the kid's rooms up and get them ready. I even vacuumed. Now granted, his house was nice, but if definitely did not have a woman's touch to it. While I was cleaning, I heard him talking to his mother on the phone, whom I have continued to keep a very close relationship with. I asked him for the phone, he gave it to me, and I said, "Heyyyyyyy"! She said, "Mommy Stink, what are you doing over there"? I said, "Oh nothing, cleaning up". She said, "that's right, and get any of them little heffers things out the house". I laughed, and said, I'm going to clean. I kept the cleaning very minimal, that day. Brandon suggested that we all go to breakfast, but I told him that it was best that I go home, so that I can check on my apartment. Plus, I wanted to check to see if Peter had been there, which I was sure he wasn't because he never called me the whole time that I was gone. I got the kids together and headed home. I loved my apartment, it was very cute, cozy, and always felt like home. When I opened the door, and stepped in, I felt so weird. It felt like I was in a stranger's house. All of the coziness, and comfort that I once felt, was gone. It felt empty, even with all of my things there. I felt like I walked in the wrong house. Instantly, I felt empty, and as soon as I felt that feeling of emptiness, Brandon texted me. I read the text and it said: "I want ya'll to come back. Can ya'll please come back"? I did not even hesitate, I said, "I am tired, I just need to take a nap". He said, "you can sleep here, I got the kids. Come on." That was my cue. I packed the kids up so fast that even they were confused. I said, "Ya'll wanna go back to your daddy's and watch cable"? (Messing with Peter, my cable was off). My daughter said, "That's weird, we just left daddy's. Are you going to go"? Knowing d@mn well that I was going, I said, "I mean…do you want me to go"? She said, "YES". I said "Come on!! Hurry up"!! I was rushing them, we did not have time to waste. I was picking up their toys and throwing them in the toy bins so fast. LOL. From the time we got in the door, to the time we got back to his house, I swear it was 15 minutes. When we pulled up, I didn't knock or ring the doorbell. I just put the code in and went in as if I was home. I heard him yell downstairs, "Kiiiiii". "It's me", I yelled back. I went upstairs and flopped in the bed as if it were mine. He immediately went into daddy mode and started to get the kids in order. "Come on ya'll, let Mommy take a nap". I knew that I was tired, but I was "tired" tired. There had been so much weight on me, I just needed some rest. I fell into a deep sleep. When I woke up, I felt like I was on vacation in an island somewhere. My body had not felt this rested in years. I felt restored. This was a breath of fresh air. I could smell food in the air. He cooked dinner for me. I took in a deep breath and exhaled and said, "thank you God". He came to the room serving me a plate of homemade food. He is an amazing cook! He can truly throw down. He made me fried chicken, meatloaf, fresh mashed potatoes, and broccoli. I appreciated this meal more than any meal that he had ever prepared. I had not had a man cook for me since he and I broke up. Peter never cooked, he could not cook. I savored every bite of that meal. After I ate, I went back to sleep. This was such a treat. I spent the night again, and enjoyed another night of rest. Peter never called, which meant he still wasn't at my apartment. The next morning, Brandon got back into his Daddy routine and got the kids together to drop them off at school. It was Monday, which was usually my day to drop them off, but he insisted on taking them. When he left to drop them off I was able to lay in his bed and take in everything that was going on. I seriously could not believe I was in his house, let alone had spent the night two nights in a row. He asked me not to leave and to wait for him to get back. He got back a lot quicker than I thought, I guess he wanted to make sure that I did not leave. He told me that he had to go get his car looked at and asked me if I would go with him. Usually, I work on Mondays, but this particular Monday, I did not have any clients on my book. I rode with him to get his car looked at out Tysons, VA. Once we left the mechanic shop, he asked me did I want to go to the mall to eat and go shopping. I accepted the food part, but denied the shopping part. When we got to the mall, he insisted that he buy me something. This was not out the norm for Brandon, he loves to take me shopping. Before I knew it, he had me in Louis Vuitton, Gucci, Saks, and whatever other high-end store he saw. "Ki, try these on. These would look cute on your feet" he said. I tried on some boots that I really liked, I said, "I love these". "Aight bet, Miss, can you box these up for her. We going to get these", he said. I said, "Actually, no they really hurt my feet, I don't want them. Lets look around some more". I had to say something to stop him from buying them. When we went into Gucci I saw these glitter shoes that I loved and could NOT deny it. "OMG!! Now these, I absolutely LOVE", I said with excitement. "Aight bet, that's what we getting", he said. I convinced him that I wanted to eat and then come back, just so he would not buy them. Now, I get it, the average woman would have let him buy the shoes and been out the door. Me, yes, I love nice things. I love shoes, I love bags, I love designer things. But, at the same time, those things are not at the top of my list. I knew that Brandon had more important things to take care of and I wanted him to get his priorities out the way first. We headed to get something to eat. "You want to go to Cheesecake Factory?", he asked. "That's sounds good", I said. We walked over to the restaurant and once we entered I was thinking to myself, "dag this looks just like the one we went to in Baltimore on our first date". Soon as that thought ended, he said "Don't this one look like the one we used to go to in Baltimore"? I said, "Brandon, I swear to God, I was just thinking the SAME thing". We got seated and instantly started to talk. It was like we were on our first date when we were 19 all over again. We talked about everything under the sun. This was the first time that we were able to truly catch up in almost 2 years. We drank, laughed, and enjoyed each other's company. When we finished eating and left, we went outside to talk more. He asked me did I want to go back and get the Gucci shoes. I explained to him that I really liked them, but I knew there were some things that he needed to take care of. One of those things was getting his house in order. Again, it was really nice, but it was missing something, I just couldn't put my finger on it. It was just a house, it needed to be a home. So, I said, "how about you give me the money that you were going to spend on the shoes, and let me go shopping for your house and decorate your living room". When I first got to his house a few days before he asked me could I help him with decorating and getting the kids rooms together. He knew just like my friends knew that I was the "Black Martha". He agreed with giving me the money to help get his house in order. Then he said, "See Ki, this is why I love you. All these other women I've been dealing with would have went in that mall and let me go broke. They'd be so caught up in bags and shoes. They don't care about getting my house together. You have never asked me for things or money, that's why I want to do these things for you. These women just see me and see I got a little bit of money, a house, a business, and they are after that. They don't genuinely care about me. They just want me to always do something for them. You have been there since day one. Back when I was driving the broke down jeep with no money. You were there when I didn't have nothing. If I was to go broke today, these women would not want to have anything to do with me". This was just a snippet of what he said. I have always loved Brandon for who he was. I was there from the very beginning when neither one of us had anything. I watched every success of his grow from a seed in the ground. I was there. I am not attached to materialistic things. Again, yes I love nice clothes, bags, shoes, etc., however, I would much rather put my money into my home. I like to come home to a nice place, this is what inspires me to do more. I want my home to feel like a vacation home when I enter it. As far as I am concerned I should not get that happy feeling only when I am on vacation. I want home to feel like a breath of fresh air. I was more excited at the thought of helping him get his home together. We left the mall, and went to pick up the kids, together. The kids were so excited! "Mommy! Daddy!" I could not deny the joy on their faces. This is day 3 of me coming over, I did not want to overstay my welcome. I told him that I was going to take the kids and head home. He asked me again to stay and not to leave. It didn't take much convincing, I made up my mind up that I was staying another night. This was the first night that Peter had called me while I wasn't home. He called me, and I pulled his famous move on him. I did not answer. I just texted him back "my phone on 2%". He used to say that when he was out doing whatever with whoever, and I always thought "if that is the case, doesn't it require less battery to just talk"? He called again, I ignored, again. This time, I called Britt and told her to text him from her phone as if we were out. She texted him, "Hey this Ki. I'm out with Britt and its

147

loud in here, I will call you when I leave". I did not care if it made sense or not, I was over him and his games. He later texted me and said, "You probably not out with Brittany, you're probably at Brandon's house". I covered my mouth and laughed. This was not the first time that he insinuated something like this, this was just the first time that it was actually true. The next day was the first day that I did not spend the whole day with Brandon. He gave me the money to shop for his house and I was excited to get the day started. It was my off day so I was able to move freely. My first stop was to my cousin's house. No one had any idea where I had been for the past few days. When I got to my cousins house I was smiling from ear to ear. I said, "Guess where I have been for the past few days?" She would have never guessed so I spilled the beans, "At BRANDONS"! I told her everything that I just shared with you, and she was ecstatic! She said, "I could just give you a kiss right now as happy as I am". Her eyes were getting watery and everything. She could not stand Peter, she actually said she "hated" him. One day she called me and said she was walking home and could not stop thinking about him, and the thought of him made her so mad. She said it was a feeling about him that she just could not shake. Once I told her every last detailed, we both excitedly hopped in the car and headed to shop for Brandon's house. I was in pure heaven and so was she. We ended up in Burlington's first, and we tore that store up. I found all kinds of things that would accent the furniture that he had. There was one pillow that I loved and when I showed my cousin, she said, "No". It was a blue pillow that said, "family". She said, "Don't get that pillow. Are you decorating for you, or for him? He is going to think you are trying to move in". I interrupted her and said, "Girl! Please, I am not thinking about moving in. At the end of the day, when he comes home to his kids, that IS his "family". We went back and forth, but I got the pillow anyway. After hitting the other stores, I was ready to get to the decorating part. I dropped her off, drove past my house, didn't even stop, and headed straight to Brandon's house. I put the door code in, turned off the alarm, and continued through the house as if I was not a guest. I turned the music on and before I started to decorate, I cleaned that house from top to bottom. I was doing dishes, mopping, sanitizing, bleaching, sweeping, and dusting. I found myself on my hands and knees cleaning the floors, showers and bathrooms. I opened the bathroom cabinet and saw some evidence of previous women he had dealt with, which consisted of: pads, razors, and other feminine items. In my head I figured maybe I should just leave them there. Then, I felt something over me and I swept everything up in one sweep and bagged it all up along with a few pieces of clothing I found in the closet. Once I got rid of any remembrance of his past dealings, I took the small plastic bag and opened the garage door and sat it on top of the trashcan. By the time I finished cleaning, the house smelled amazing. It smelled as if a maid had come in to clean. Now, it was time to decorate. This was my favorite part. I got so much joy out of both the cleaning and the decorating, but there was over joy in decorating. Hours later, I stood back and looked at the work I had done like, "wow". I was amazed myself. I checked the time and saw that it was getting closer to the time for him to pick the kids up from school. I went upstairs to take a hot shower and change into one of the new outfits I had bought. I had been buying clothes because I left my apartment so quickly I didn't have time to pack. I headed to the kitchen to make one of his favorite meals that I make, baked spaghetti. Once that was done, I headed up to the bathroom to run him a hot bath. I lit some candles, added some bubbles, and turned the lights off in the bathroom. I have always done things like this for him. I positioned myself to be in the kitchen when they came in. I heard the kids talking as they came in, "is mommy here"? When they came up the stairs our daughter was like, "OH MY GAWD!! MOM! It looks sooooo nice in here". I stood back and looked around admiring my work again, "Ya'll like it"? Brandon looked and rubbed his nose with his thumb with a smirk on his face (this is what he does when he is so excited and tries to compose himself). "Aye Ki, I can't lie. It looks really nice in here"!! I walked him upstairs to his room, which I had redone as well. He absolutely loved it! Once he got to the bathroom, I told him to relax and take a bath. I had wine out for him as well. While he soaked in the tub, I headed downstairs to finish the final touches on the baked spaghetti. His mom called in the process. "What you over there doing? Did you get them hookers mess out his house"? I said, "yep. I cleaned up"! She knew the type of cleaning that I was talking about and that made her happy. She asked where he was and I said, "Oh he is just upstairs soaking in the bath that I ran for him. Would you believe the man ain't never been in the tub since he bought the house"? She said, "That's a d@mn shame". Not only had I not had a chance to truly relax and get catered to while we were broken up, but neither had he. I could see the sense of relief on his face once he came downstairs from bathing. I pretended as if "my work here is done" and attempted to "go home". This is when he said, "Ki, I don't want you to leave. I want you to be here with me everyday. I got this house, hoping that you would come back. I thought about you when I got this house. I don't ever want you to leave. I want to just do this with you. Please stay. You can get rid of your apartment and come here with me. I'll pay whatever to help you get rid of it. You can stay here and stack your bread. You can just pay the utilities". I instantly decided that his home would now be my home too. I could not believe that my decision-making was so effortless. At this point I don't remember much about Peter calling. I know he called a few times, most of the time I ignored him. Once I confirmed that I had a new home, I finally answered one of his texts. I texted him and told him that he needed to figure out his own living situation because I was moving with my cousin to save some money. I didn't tell him the truth, because it wasn't his business. He would find out soon enough what was really going on. It was a new beginning for Brandon and I, and it was refreshing to be back in each other's lives. During this time we had some of the deepest conversations. One night we were in the middle of talking and he gave me this funny look. I said, "What's wrong"? He started to look weird and his body was shaking a little. I got scared and jumped off the bed to the floor where he was. He just burst into tears and said, "I JUST LOVE YOU SO MUCH! And I am so happy that you are here! I can't believe that you are here. I did all of this for you". I could not hold back the tears so at this point I was crying too. We both laid on the floor crying like two newborn babies in each other's arms. Once we dried up our tears, we decided to go get something to eat. As we were eating at the restaurant, I looked at the time and realized it was 12:00 a.m. and it was Rence's birthday. I suggested that we both call her to wish her a happy birthday. When she answered the phone I yelled "HAPPY BIRTHDAY", she said "Thanks". I said, "My friend wanted to wish you a happy birthday too"! I could hear the irritation in her voice, she said, "Oh....kay"? She said it more in the tone of a question than answer. I put the phone on speaker and passed Brandon the phone. "Happy Birthday Rence' Roo", he said. She was like, "Brandon? What in the h3ll is going on!? Is this a birthday joke? What are you doing with Ki"? I grabbed the phone and said "GIRLLLL we back together. I moved in the house and everything"! She was so confused. But, she was happy and said, "wait is this my birthday gift? If so I am so happy". This was just the beginning to all the people we were going to surprise with this news. Rence' birthday dinner was a day or so later, guess who I showed up to the dinner with on my arm? Brandon! The family had not got word yet. When I sat down, everyone looked confused, yet happy. The all said "hi" to Brandon but no one acted weird because Brandon was family at the end of the day. When Brandon got up to go to the bathroom, my grandfather whispered to me; "So you and Brandon back together"? I said, "yep! That other dude? Yeah he had to go. So, yes, me and Brandon are back together, oh and I moved in the house with him". It was like I had given everyone the "wake up" call they were patiently waiting on me to receive. My grandfather said, "That's good. Real good. It's good when you can keep your family together". I also told him the future plans that we had to get married. Yes, we definitely discussed getting married as I was very adamant about not getting back together if that was not the plan. I was NOT about to waste my time all over again. There was no such thing as rushing to me in this particular situation. Granted we had been broken up for almost 2 years, but, before that we had been together for over a decade and had 2 kids together. Further more, we had known each other for 14 years. A situation like that can not possibly be rushed when it comes back around. Our next stop in the days to follow would be to my father's side of the family. We went over to my grandmothers to tell her, my father, my aunts and whoever else was there that day. Everyone was so happy. We went upstairs to tell my aunt that I am close in age with. I said, "You want to meet my new boyfriend"? She said, "Bye Rickia"! She was not for the games that day. Brandon came walking up behind her and said, "Hey Mu"! She turned around and said, "BRANDON"!? We told her that we were back together and she could not hide her excitement, she started crying real tears. She said, "Omg I am really crying, I am so happy". Next, we went downstairs to tell my father. He thought we were lying. Once he realized that we were serious, he said, "You know what you going to have to do next right? You are going to have to marry her". He suggested what we were already thinking, and that was, that we go off to get married at the Justice of Peace. Both of us agreed that we were planning on taking the steps to get married in the near future. This time around, we were not in it to play games. Before our first engagement, I made sure to tell Brandon that if he planned on asking me to marry him, he needed to talk to the men in my life first and get their blessing. He respected my wishes and talked to both my father and grandfather and got their blessings. We first got engaged, we stayed engaged for years, until we broke up. I stopped calling him my fiancé once we had been engaged past 3 years. Neither one of us were ready at the time. I stopped wearing my ring because it was embarrassing to me after having our second child, living together, and still not going anywhere. This time around, I was not going to give him the time extension that I had before. Sometimes, he would avoid my family to avoid the questions, especially when it came to going to my family's church. My grandfather, uncles, and sometimes even other members would randomly pull him aside when I wasn't around. They would ask, "When are you going to marry her"? I'm not sure what his response would be, but the question being asked alone was embarrassing to me. When we broke up for the last time before getting back together this time, I vented to my grandfather about all the things he and I had went through. One thing that my grandfather said that hit me hard was when he said, "I was very disappointed in Brandon for not marrying you. He came to me and asked me to marry you and he never kept his word. Then he had another baby with you and still didn't honor that, that's when I was done". The men in my family are very protective of me and saw me worthy of being a wife, and not just someone's "baby's momma" or "shack up" partner. With me allowing him back into my life, it was much different. This wasn't our typical break up for a short period of time and get right back together. This time, it took much more for him to finally get himself together. That 2 year break up was much needed. Him seeing me getting my own place, and furthermore a new "man" in the picture was essential to the wake up call that he needed. He never thought that he stood another chance, neither did I. But, with this final chance starring him in the face, it was either he could be all in or all out, forever. I did not realize how much our love and relationship impacted others around us. We stressed a lot of them out during our relationship. One person in particular was our friend, Cristi. She is that friend that takes on the issues of her friends. When we were going through it, she went through it too. She came over many, many times to counsel us through our issues. She was like the unofficial third wheel to our relationship. When we would break up, she would always try to fix it. One time we broke up, he went to live with her. She would call me like, "Ki, please let my brother come back. Please!! He can not live here with me anymore. He needs to be home with yall". Or if she was upset with him, she would call me going off, "do you know this n!gg@ took my fuc#!ng clothes out the washer and put my expensive shirt on the FLOOR"!? I would be on the other end like, "Cristi, I don't know. He can't come here though". She was so used to us going through break ups to make ups, that even she never thought that she would see the day that we parted ways for real. During the final breakup, she and I fell off. She was upset with me for not telling her about the "new friend" that I had. I explained to her that I did not ever want to put

her in a position where she felt uncomfortable. I knew that
Brandon would go over to her house and cry and vent to her. I did
not want him over there doing so with the guilt of her knowing
that I had moved on to be on her heart. She respected my decision
and thanked me for being so thoughtful. I think of all the people,
she took the breakup just as hard as Brandon. She and I stopped
talking eventually during the break. Funny thing is, now I honestly
can't remember why, it was very petty on my end. So petty that I
could not even explain to her why. It wasn't the pettiness that set
her off, it was the fact that in the process of me being upset, I
blocked her number. She was trying to text me to make a hair
appointment and realized she was blocked when she attempted to
call, after realizing that her messages were not going through. I
swear she cursed me out for weeks with one too may long text
messages calling me all types of b!tc#es. It made her more mad
when I would reply, "ok", or some biblical verse on an evil tongue.
When Brandon and I got back together, we still weren't talking. His
mom always said, "out of everyone, ya'll need to apologize to Cristi
because yall took her through the most". She carried our
relationship just as if it was hers. She too was drained and tired.
The next day after going over to my father's side to share the news,
we planned to go see Cristi. I told Brandon to act like I was his
friend and tell her that he wanted her to meet me. I stood in the
hallway and listened to the whole conversation. He walked in and
said, "Aye Rai, I want you to meet my friend". She came out and
said, "Son, no. I'm sorry. I can't. I don't want to meet your friend".
He said, "but she is in the hallway". She said, "Brandon, I don't

care. I don't want to meet her". She then went in the room to tell her boyfriend to come and talk to Brandon because she did not want to meet any of his friends. As she was coming back from her room, Brandon said, "She is coming in". She was ready to curse him out, until she looked up and saw me. She was stuck! She said, "Wait! What is going on!! Wait! Wait!! What does this mean? Please tell me what does this mean? Does this mean I HAVE MY FAMILY BACK? Please say yes, OMG"! She was covering her mouth with tears in her eyes waiting for us to answer. I said, "YES". She started to scream and burst into tears thanking God. The kids were there in the room and they came out to join our 3-way hug. We were all crying, even the kids were crying. It was a very emotional moment. It was like we were all back like we never left. She looked at Brandon and said, "Man Joe, you got her back Brandon! You got her back"! She was like a proud sister. She was proud of him for making the necessary changes to get me back. We went back into our family routine that day. When went and got some crabs, drinks, and laughed and hugged the night away. This was just the beginning of many surprises. The next big event for me was my salon grand opening party. I had not talked to Peter, but strangely, he called me on the day of my grand opening. I guess he had been watching my instagram posts. I answered to make sure he was not going to try to pull any stunts on my big day. Soon as I answered the first thing out of his mouth was, "what time is the grand opening today"? I said, "you are not invited". He said, "Man what?! I am coming! This is something that we been working on". I stopped him in his tracks, "WE? Boy you ain't help me with nothing"! We went back and forth for about 5 minutes. "Why would you do this on the day that I found my mother dead?", he said. I stopped him and reassured him that this was not the day that he found his mother dead. Oddly, I remembered that day and date very vividly, but I guess his vision was a little cloudy. Things a manipulator does, I'm telling ya, so extreme. Their goal in life is to make you feel guilty, in hopes that they may be able to get what they want in the end. Failed attempt on his end. That didn't work. I reiterated that he was NOT to come. Before he hung up, he said, "man I'm coming anyway. I will see you later". Immediately after getting off of the phone with him, I went into a full anxiety attack. I instantly felt an outer body experience as if I was not alive and that I was dreaming. Anxiety will rob you from an entire experience. This was a big day for me and I was robbed of that after that phone call that triggered my anxiety. The rest of the morning, I spent worrying about how the day would end. Peter was still under the impression that I was living with a family member. He would soon enough find out the truth, along with the rest of the world. I asked all the guest to wear jean and white. Brandon and I went out and got matching outfits. That day would be the day that guest that we had not visited in the previous days would find out that we were "baaacckkk". Before leaving the house, he took a picture of me sitting on the trunk of my car with my glitter Gucci shoes on (yes he surprised me and went back to get them as a gift for my grand opening). I posted it on instagram and the caption read "Life is Gucci", and that it was. While I was prepping for the grand opening, Peter called me back with urgency in his voice.

"Aye, let me ask you a question, and I want you to be very honest with me. Who bought you them Gucci shoes? Brandon"? I smirked at the fact that he knew how to answer his own question. He had offered me a few items of his merchandise, but I have always declined the offer. No shade, but I don't go out my way to wear anything fake. I'm not going to have on or buy fake designer just to say its "designer". He knew that most of the bags and shoes that I have had in the past were gifts from Brandon, so he kind of knew what was up. I responded to his question by saying, "You are worried about the wrong things. It's not your business who bought them. You ain't buy them. That's all you need to know". He got very emotional and started threating to come up to the grand opening, and then he hung up. His threats were alarming, so I went back in the salon to tell Brandon and my father that he was threating to come up there. My father is not the one for threats, his answer was simple, "let the n!gg@ come up here. I got something for him if he come. He ain't going to do $h!t". The grand opening ended great. I had my mother call Peter and convince him that there would be a lot of women there with hair loss getting wigs put on, and they wouldn't want a man seeing them. Thank God that worked because I didn't have time for any drama on my big day. Later that night, my father posted a picture of me and Brandon and it said, "my daughter and her boyfriend". I don't know how the world found his page that night, but everyone knew that we were back together, and for us we were back and better like never before. I think Peter was the first to get word and he went off calling and texting me with worst threats. It was time that I file some paper work on him, I planned to get a restraining order on him as soon as I could. That night Brandon and I were flooded with calls, texts, and messages congratulating us. No news gets around faster than news on social media. Brandon being at the grand opening was like adding the icing to my cake. He had been helping me the entire time by giving me money to get things for the shop. He purchased my first shop sign, paid for the guys to come paint, and whatever else I needed to get the shop together. He has always wanted to see me win. I thank God for him, it was him that helped get me to where I now stood, in my salon working for myself. I was able to quit my government job because he gave me the green light. He said, "You can quit your job. I am going to give you 3 years to figure out this hair thing, if you don't figure it out in 3 years, you are going to have to find a job". He helped lead me to my dream of becoming a self-employed hairstylist. Us coming together right in time for the grand opening was perfect. I felt like I got to share it all with who I started with, and that is what I ultimately wanted. He respected my business and he has always poured into me and my business. We have been each other's biggest fans since day one. I felt there was a shift coming in the atmosphere. This wasn't just a win for me, this was a win for US. He was very proud of me. It's a different type of proud when you were there with a person from the very beginning. When you get to see someone start from the very bottom and work their way to the top, it's an amazing feeling. I guess he felt like I did when I first came to his house. I was so proud, like wow, he really did this! Not only did he do it, but he did it against all odds. We both mainly got to where we were with each other, and with more things against us than for us. No matter what lemons life threw at us, we managed to make lemonade every time. Some people allow their adversities to hinder them, for us, we used them as our strength. Before my Uncle gave me the opportunity to come and take over the salon, I went through hell. I was barely making it when Brandon and I broke up. I was not living paycheck to paycheck, I was literally living day by day. My bank account went into the negative every single week. I used to drive to work everyday crying. I would often play "This is my season" by William Murphy, and sing it with tears in my eyes and on my shirt. I stayed faithful. I knew that my time was coming, I knew there was light at the end of the tunnel, but I also knew that I would have to be completely broken down to be rebuilt into who God called me to be. The sowing part of the struggle can bring some of the most trying times of your life. The sowing may bring us pain, but the reaping of good seeds can bring a peace and happiness that I could never put into words. I knew that everything was "working, together, for my good". No matter what I faced, I learned to turn to God and say "it's good" even when it was bad. I had no idea what God was going to do for me, but with all that I went through, I knew that it would be nothing short of amazing. Like the song says, "I don't care what your circumstances are, its already getting better".

9 HAPPY CLIENT
GODS PLAN IS ALWAYS BETTER

I was still overwhelmed with all the amazing things that were
happening for me. I got rid of Peter, got back with Brandon,
moved in with Brandon, had my salon grand opening, and the next
thing I needed was complete peace. There were still attachments to
Peter because his things were still in my apartment. I started
moving my things out a little at a time. I informed him that he
needed to come get his things as well but, we needed to schedule a
day and time. My cousin was very helpful with helping me move
things out of the apartment. One day we were in there packing, and
something told me to go back to the door to put the chain on and I
did. Less than 5 minutes after putting the chain on, I heard
someone attempt to open the door. It was Peter! My heart dropped
to the floor, I was really scared. He said, "Helloooooooo.
Hellllooooo". My cousin and I both got quiet, I almost walked out
the patio door, that's how scared I was. Initially I did not want to
be on the bottom floor of my apartment, but it was in a really nice

neighborhood, and later I appreciated having multiple exits in case of an emergency. This was an emergency to me. He yelled back through the door asking me if I could open the door because he just wanted to come in to get something. I told him that I had no problem with him getting his things, but he could not come in without a police escort. I picked up the phone and called the police immediately and explained the situation to them, and they said that they would come to escort him. I was so scared waiting on them to come. I have seen it on the news and T.V. one too many times. The crazy ex comes back to talk to the girlfriend, and next thing you know he shoots her, strangles her, or even sets her on fire. I was not about to take him popping up to my house lightly. This was serious, and I was letting him know that I wasn't about to play games with him. I let him know that the police was on their way, and he could wait in the hallway until they got there. Once they came, I went to get the clothes that he was asking for and handed them to him at the door, and he left. I thank God that I listened to what he was telling me. I always say that I struggle with hearing his voice, but as I am typing, I am thinking. That "something said" was God telling me. It was no accident that God had told Amy to warn me to leave him alone. Once he left, I was ready to hurry up and be done for the day, I was afraid of him coming back. Before he left, we made arrangements for him to come a few days later to pick up all of his things. That day could not come fast enough, I was ready for anything that was attached to him to be out of my life and for GOOD. When he came to get the remainder of his things, I had my cousin with me again. He and his uncle pulled up in a moving truck. I left the door unlocked and sat in the car while they moved everything that was his out. It took him about an hour. He came back to the car and said, "Oh. I need that ring back too". I wanted to laugh in his face, but I waited until he walked off to go in the house to get the ring. My cousin and I burst out laughing. I said "Girl, he can have that little ring". I did not want it. I had no reason for it. I'm sure by now, that ring is on someone else's finger. Check your finger girl! It looks like that ring that is always circulating on the gram. You know the mall ring that could be an earring too? Yes! That ring! So yeah, I had no interest in holding his ring hostage. I kindly gave it back and prayed that I would never see him again in my life. That day was the last day we saw each other. Once I filed a restraining order on him, I change my number. I wanted to make sure that I cut off any ties that I could think of with him off, and I did. It was hard for me to focus on my business at this time, I couldn't find the strength. There was a lot of weight on me from all the good and bad things that had happened. I went to a doctor to discuss my concerns of not feeling energized, and my anxiety. I told her everything that had happened within the previous weeks. She said, "You need a vacation". I said, "yes! I do. Maybe that is the perfect medicine". After that conversation, I went to the store and was talking to Brandon on the phone. I told him that I really just needed to get away real quick for a vacation. He asked me where I wanted to go. He said, "just name it, and we are going to go there". I said, "well you know I always have talked about Jamaica. I would loovvvveeee to go there". He said his favorite line, "ight bet". I know he wasn't making any broken promises. The next day, I was at work and he texted me, "check your email". I checked my email and there it was, the confirmation email for our trip to Jamaica! We were going to Jamaica!! I was super excited. I couldn't help but think about what I have always told him about Jamaica. I used to say, "When we get married, I just want to go off to an island and get married. Maybe somewhere like Jamaica. I don't want a big wedding. I don't want any bridesmaids, I just want my sister as my maid of honor. Then, we can have a reception later back home." I got a little giddy at the thought of that conversation. What are the chances of that happening? There was no way. I erased the thought and took in the excitement of taking a trip to Jamaica. I was so excited and told my clients about the trip he had planned and they were excited as well. I began getting prepared for the trip in the weeks to follow. I started to order things for the trip right away. Brandon instructed me to bring something white for an all white party, so I made sure to order a white dress as well. I was finally settled in to my new home with Brandon. I got rid of the apartment, put my old furniture in storage, and moved all of me and the kid's things to the house. We were operating with complete structure, we continued to do our drop-offs and pick-up's with the kids on our original designated days. The day of the trip could not come fast enough!! The night before the trip, I did not sleep at all. I was too excited. The next day we got to the airport, checked our bags, went through customs, and finally was able to sit down and catch a breather. We sat and talked about how excited we were to go to Jamaica. The week ahead, we confirmed that we would go to the Justice of Peace and get married on our original anniversary date from when we first became a couple at the age of 19. This also happened to be the original date for our wedding that was planned for 2013. That date was December 15th. We were leaving on a Saturday, and planned to come back that Thursday to go to the Justice of Peace that Friday to get married. Once we boarded the plane and everyone was seated, I heard them call me on the intercom; "Rickia Taylor, please report to the front". I had just gotten my passport, I did not need it when I went to Puerto Rico, so I had no idea why they were calling me. I thought that maybe it was something wrong with my passport, I got up nervously to attempt to walk to the front. Brandon said, "Why they calling you? You want me to go with you"? I said, "No. I am fine, let me see what they want. He got up and followed me anyway. The closer I got to the front, he started pulling me saying, "Ki. Ki. Ki." I ignored him and kept walking because I did not want to hold anyone else up from their trip. When I got to the front, he was right there with me. Then he looked at me and that is when I was thinking, "this is not happening". The flight attendant gave it away by saying, "we have a proposal going on board of the aircraft". I was completely shocked. Before I could take in what she said, Brandon was on his knee. He told me how much he loved me and asked me would I marry him. I could barely get it out because I was crying so hard, but I shook my head and said, "YES"! We hugged, then kissed. Everyone on the flight was cheering and clapping and even taking pictures. We have the perfect footage of the proposal, thanks to one of the people on board. I had no idea that Brandon had talked to a few people right before we boarded the flight. I remember seeing him go to the front desk to ask a question, but I thought that was all he was doing, asking a question. I had no idea that he was planning the proposal of my life! I could not believe that he proposed again. I was truly amazed. I was on a high of happiness that I could not even begin to describe. When we got back to our seats, I kept crying, all I could say is "BRANDON!! BRANDON!! WOOOWWW". His timing was impeccable. He knew that I hated flying so him getting me this excited right before taking off, drifted my mind on the happiness of being engaged versus the fear of flying. This proposal was one that I was not ashamed of, I was ready to immediately share it with the world. My girlfriend Amy later said, "I know you were surprised, because you look crazy as h3ll". I did not care how crazy I looked, I was too happy, looking crazy was the least of my concerns. I shared the video on instagram and did not care what anyone thought. My sister added some music to it and that made it even more special. Apparently, she knew that he was planning on proposing. Once we landed in Jamaica, it was time for us to celebrate, and we did just that. I wanted to make sure that I enjoyed every last moment of that trip. I wanted the time to go slow so that I could savor the moment. I mean, we partied, drank, ate good, laughed, joked, and just enjoyed each other's company like never before. In the days to follow we continued to do those same things over and over again. I told him that I wanted to go to a "REAL" Jamaican party. We left the resort and I got to experience a REAL Jamaican party, I had a ball. Everyday was fun. My sister had the kids while we were away so I was able to facetime them to check on them. Most of the time I did not have service, so I wasn't able to talk to them but once a day. I was finally able to get the break that I needed. Everything around me was nothing short of beautiful and very relaxing. I am convinced that everyday of life should feel like a vacation. We met a couple of ladies on the elevator and asked how long they would be there, they said that they were staying for a week. I looked at Brandon and said, "I would love to be here for a week, that would be perfect". It rained everyday that we had been there at this point. There was not one full day of sunshine, it literally rained all day everyday. We continued to do the excursions and hang at the bars outside, even with the rain. Brandon got more and more irritated the more it rained. I asked him on several occasions, "What's wrong"? His response was very predictable after the second time of asking him, "This rain s#!t is blowing me". I said, "Yeah, it's blowing me too. Yeah it's raining, but at the end of the day, we are in JAMAICA"! I was just grateful to be there. The rain wasn't going to stop me from enjoying myself in Jamaica. The days went by so fast, before I knew it, it was time to go. Brandon instructed me to go to the room and pack our things, and to make sure I had our passports. He went to take care of some credit card fraud that was going on with his cards. I stayed in the room and packed everything and kept reminding myself , "MAKE SURE YOU HAVE THE PASSPORTS"! I had everything packed and went to double check for the passports, they were not there. Panic did not settle in yet as I took my time to look very carefully. I knew that they were in my purse, but from some odd reason, I could not find them. Once I realized that they were not appearing, I had to call Brandon to be the bearer of bad news. I prepared myself for him to go off. He answered the phone and I told him that I could not find the passports. He seemed to be a little upset, but not the way I had imagined that he would be. His reaction made me feel like there was something going on. I went to meet him in the lobby with our bags, as I approached him, I asked him had he seen the passports. He tried to hide his smile and said, "No, I can't believe you lost them". By then, I knew something was up. I know him so well that I know when he is lying or hiding something from me. I just went with the flow. He said that we would have to wait a few more days for them to send us our new passports. We were going to stay a little longer than expected. I apologized about the mishap of me losing the passports, but I also told him that I was not mad about being in Jamaica for four more days. He said that he went to the front desk and demanded that they upgrade us for the inconvenience they caused us when someone tried to scam his credit card. I sent out mass texts to all the clients that I had on the book for the remainder of the week letting them know that I was sorry, but due to circumstances beyond my control, I needed to reschedule. Everyone was very understanding. Once I got confirmation on rescheduled dates for my clients, I was ready to enjoy the next few days in every way I could. I was super excited. He said, "With us being here until Sunday now, we won't be able to make it to the Justice of Peace for the 15th". I said, "It's ok, I am just happy to be here. We can always go when we get back". The Justice of Peace wasn't going anywhere, although the perfect

169

wedding date 12/15/17 for us was. We then headed to our upgraded new room, the room was breathtaking. It sat right on the water. It had an outdoor shower, a huge hot tube, a bungalow, and a few other perks that the other room did not have. We met up with a couple of his friends that had come as well, they just happened to pop up in Jamaica. This wasn't unusual to me because they are always taking trips. I was soaking in every moment of this trip because I needed a break. This trip helped me restore peace and balance back into my life. I still could not believe that I was not only in Jamaica, but that I was there with Brandon. Thursday night, we chilled. We sat up for a while in bed, laughing and talking. Brandon kept looking at me saying, "Do you really love me? I really love you. I just love you so much". The way that he said it concerned me because he was crying and sounded like he was hiding something. I even asked him was there something that he needed to tell me, because I felt like he wanted to tell me something but he was scared. He tried his best to reassure me that he wasn't hiding anything for me, but my gut told me that there was something still. That entire night, the "I love you's" never stop, and neither did his tears. I think he probably cried himself to sleep that night. I went to sleep wondering if he was hiding something. The next morning, I was awakened by the sun. It literally rained every single day that we were in Jamaica up until this point. I was so excited that I woke Brandon up to show him that we finally got some sun on our vacation. Him seeing the sun made him smile from ear to ear. It was December 15th, and we both wished each other a Happy Anniversary. When we laid back down, he looked at me and said, "Today our lives are about to change forever". He then passed me the room key and it said "Honey Moon Suite". I looked at it like "Oookkay". He said, "You still don't get it do you"? I said, "No". I really had no idea what he was insinuating. I got what the key said, but we were upgraded, so us being in a Honey Moon Suite, may have been the best suite to upgrade us to. He usually likes to lay around before completely getting up to get ready, but this day, he hopped out the bed and started to get ready early. Before getting out the bed, he said, "a few people are going to come and help you get ready. I will meet up with you later". I love surprises, so I did not ask 100 questions about what was really going on, I just decided to go with the flow. After he got out the shower he asked me to pass him the brush out of the suitcase, when I opened up a zipper to see if it was in there, I gasped really loud. He said, "what is wrong"? I said, "Nothing, I thought I saw a bug". I knew he had something up his sleeve when I saw the passports in that zipper pocket. I didn't want him to feel like he had to tell me what was going on at that point, so I decided not to tell him. When he left, I sat in the bed and took it all in. I had the patio window opened and just smiled at the sun and listened to the waves of the ocean. I said my morning prayer and I was very specific, "God, I don't know what is going on today, but I pray that I feel alive in every moment. I pray that I get to fully enjoy and savor each and every minute of today. Please remove the spirit of anxiety. I do not want to feel like I am dreaming or not here today. I want to have a beautiful day and truly get to bask in all the amazing things that are to come with today. Lord, I thank you in

advance, amen". I trusted that it was already done and that God
was going to answer my prayer. I had all the faith that I needed. I
walked around the room, touching things, smelling the air, feeling
the sheets, stretching to the sun, and simply holding my chest
hugging myself with all sorts of happiness. The feeling that I was
feeling was pure joy and gratefulness. Brandon had only been out
of the room for 5 minutes before he came back knocking. I ran to
the door and opened it without looking or asking who it was, as I
strutted back to the bathroom. "Can I be your bridesmaid", said
Rence'. I don't even think I even turned all the way around before I
started to scream. "OMG!!! What in the h3ll"!? I could not believe
my eyes. She showed me a button that said "bridesmaid". She said,
"girl we are getting MARRIED in a few hours"!! I could not
believe what I was even hearing. In my head I continued my prayer,
"God please let me enjoy it! Make me feel alive! I want to be able
to live in this moment! I want it to be like a dream but not feel like
a dream"! My sister is the best, she even brought me a wig that her
and my mother picked out. I had about 5 wigs on the trip, but the
one that she bought me would be perfect. It pays to be a hairstylist
on vacation. That wig was shaved on one side and long on the
other. It took a hairstylist eyes to see the potential beauty in it. I
said, "this is perfect", as I tried it on and visualized how I was
going to tweak it to make it look perfect. Weeks before I remember
she and Brandon asking how I would want to wear my hair when I
got married. I said that I wanted it to be long, but not too long, and
I wanted it to be to one side and have like a pin curl/vintage look.
That wig was perfect, they both took heed to what I said. We had a

little more time before it was time to get married. My big day was perfect. No stress, no craziness, no bride-zilla. It was chill, just like me. Rence' and I sat on the patio, kicked our feet up, ordered room service, and ate our food while watching the ocean as the time passed by. I am not a makeup girl like that, I usually pack just the basics; mascara, lipstick, lip-gloss, brow liner and eyeliner. I needed a little more for my big day. I asked my sister to go to the store on the resort to get me some makeup. She did not seem to be in a hurry at all, although now was time to actually really start moving around. Time was ticking. I had to ask her about 3 times to go before she finally decided to head for the door. Just when I thought she was going out, someone else was coming in. I was naked in the tub and I heard a familiar voice say, "Guess who is here"? It was my mother-in-law. I screamed while trying to gather my thoughts and cover my breast, vagina, and butt all at the same time. I was moving like Omarion in the "Touch" video. She said, "ahh child ain't no one looking at you, I came to do your makeup". I loosened up once I realize that she has literally seen my butt in the air two times when I gave birth to both of my children. She seen parts of me that I had not ever seen! LOL. I got out and put on one of the thick robes, complimentary of the hotel. She set up her makeup with a smile on her face. I sat there in pure joy. She said, "I am so honored to be here to do your makeup. Isn't this amazing"? I said, "yes it is, I can not believe it". This was more than a breath of fresh air for her, her son was finally ready to step up and be the man that we both prayed years ago that he would be. While she was doing my makeup, I had my eyes closed and was thinking, "this must be what it is like to be a real princess". I felt so special. I mean, yeah I see things on social media or T.V. like that happen to other people, but for it to be actually happening to me was beyond what words could ever describe. Once she finished, I got up to put my clothes on. I bent down to grab the white party dress that I had ordered online, and said, "well, I guess I will wear this", as I held it up to myself in the mirror. I turned around to show the girls, and I gasped for air. "OMG!!! Where did this come from!! Omg!! Who put this here"? When I turned to them, I couldn't miss what I saw on the bed. There it was, everything I needed, right before my eyes: the wedding dress, a veil, jewelry, a garter belt, shoes, a robe that said "wifey", a hanger that said "bride", and some flip flops that said "bride". I was speechless. I felt like Cinderella. They helped me put the dress on, and omg, it fit so perfect. I don't think anything has ever fitted me so perfect. I starred in the mirror in disbelief. A phone call to the room was received, saying that they were on their way to come pick up the bride. When I stepped out the door, my sister was right behind me holding my dress. We walked to the car that came to pick us up. As we were driving to where the services would be held, I just thanked God over and over again in my head. When we got out the car, I heard a lady come through to the other lady on the radio saying, "the playlist won't play, at this point, we are going to just have to play something else". Whatever they were trying to play, my sister was able to send to Brandon's friend just in time. The woman confirmed, "We got it!! We got the music". I was anxious to know what the music was. Once my feet hit the ground and I took my first step, I couldn't hold back the tears. Soon as I heard, "guess what I did today", my heart completely dropped!! When I was in the 8th grade, Case "Happily Ever After" was my favorite song. I said a million times back then, "when I get married, I want to get married to this song". I told Brandon the same thing when we first met at 19, and my sister definitely knew that was what I repeatedly said. Hearing that song play as I walked down the aisle confirmed that my fairytale was becoming my reality. I took slow steps to every word, "Guess what I did today, those were the words I said to you. It was last May, don't know the exact day, in my hand there was a ring. Then you told me that you love me, more than anything in your life. So I asked you would you do me, the honor of being my wife. Yesss I will", and the song continued. We all say things as a child, and plan out our dream weddings, but this WAS my dream wedding happening in real life. This was a feeling I could never explain. The closer I got, the more I could see Brandon crying. This moment was special. Everything that we had been through, all the drama, all the fights, all the good times, the laughs, the smiles, the cries and everything else that came with our relationship, was finally making sense. This is what needed to happen for God to execute his plan. We were broken before, all of those broken pieces now made this beautiful puzzle of happiness. This was pure bliss. Even with all the chaos, he was listening all along. I said I wanted an all white beach wedding on an island in Jamaica, we were there on the beach obeying the dress code. I said I didn't want any bridesmaids, just my sister, there she stood as my only bridesmaid/maid of honor. I wanted my favorite wedding song to play, Case made his way to the speakers soon as my feet hit the ground. The way I wanted my hair, perfect, it was exactly how I wanted it. With all that he took me through, this fairytale that I was in the moment of, made me let go of it all. He thought out every detail to my fairytale wedding. Even with the date of December 15th. His thinking officially made that date so much more special. He said that before he decided to do the wedding in Jamaica, he had a talk with God. He asked God that if it were meant for us to get married on that date of 2017, then when he added the numbers up it would equal 17. 17 is a very special number for us both, it is our favorite number. My birthday is May 17th and his is July 17th. After asking God to confirm with him through a numerical sign, it was confirmed! Our wedding date 12/15/17 when added together as single digits = 17. (1+2+1+5+1+7=17) In the biblical numbers 1 represents unity and 7 represents completion, this as a whole represented our marriage. This was our happy beginning. I don't think anyone other than us was excited as our daughter Marley. She was not at the wedding, but she face-timed me right after. When she saw me her entire face lit up with joy. "Mommy, you look so pretty" she said in aw. She was so happy, when she found out that we were officially married, my grandmother said that she went in the room and started crying. Marley prayed day in and day out that she would get her family back. Before that day that we all sat on the same row at church, she changed the screen saver on her phone to a picture of her, Brandon and me. I was a little sad when I saw it because, I knew that she would be disappointed because I just knew that that was never happening. When I asked her about it, she told me, "Grammies said when you really want something you have to believe it and pray for it". I reflected on that day the week after we got married. I thought, "wow, God. All this time I did not even see what you were working on". Brandon planned the whole wedding within two weeks. No one had time to plan to attend in such a short notice, but I was fine with that because we still planned on having a reception. I later found out that he was having secret meetings with my best friends Tye and Ash. They picked out my dress and everything that laid on the bed. He contacted them, met with them, and apologized to them for all that he put me through. Then he asked would they help him and they were so honored. Hearing that and seeing all the videos that my friends and family sent had me in tears. My sister asked everyone to send us special messages and she put them all on one video. Everything turned out perfect. Soon as we got back home it was almost Christmas. We were all headed together just like old times to pick out our Christmas tree. The Christmas tree is a big deal to us, but especially to Brandon and Marley. For years, before Sélah was born, this was their thing. They would always have to pick out the biggest tree. Sélah didn't remember the few years before, he was still only 3. He helped them pick the tree and I stood back and watched. I needed to soak in the moment that we were in, we were back to our traditions. When we were walking back to the truck, Marley said, "this is the best Christmas ever! We got the biggest tree! And we have our family back together"!! It was like some scene out of a movie with the perfect ending. We rode home laughing, singing, and joking. We were all so happy, now happily married. Christmas 2018 was even more special. We got a bigger tree and took pictures with matching pajamas. I posted a picture on instagram and part of the caption said, "Marley got her family back and this year WITH matching pajamas". I love my family and I love how Brandon prepared himself to be the husband that I deserved. I can honestly say that I married my best friend. I can be my complete self around him. He knows the real "Ki" and every bit of her. He adores me, from my head to my toes. I love the way that he loves me, and when we got back together, I realized how much everyone else loves the way he loves me. My family can rest at night because they know that he is going to take care of his kids and me. When I am with him, I don't have to pick up the phone and call any of the men in my family for anything that a man should do, because he is already doing it. He is the man of my dreams. No, we are not perfect, but yes we are perfect for each other. He is the one that I am willing to fight with and fight for. Everyday is not perfect, yes we argue, yes we have disagreements, yes some days we may not even "like" each other. But, at the end of the day, our love for each other is out of this world. We truly enjoy doing life together. We make each other laugh, we will go above and beyond for each other, we love to be the reason that the other person is smiling, can't no one love us like we can love us. Despite all that we have been through, I still love this man with all my heart. He has been in my life for 15 years and I look forward to the rest of my life with him. We have grown up together. Getting to where we are now required a lot of maturing, praying, fighting, and whatever else comes with making a relationship work. But you know what, even with the past, I wouldn't trade our story for any other story in the world. None of us are perfect, we are all flawed. It's not about finding someone you won't have to fight with or for, it's about finding that one that is worth the fight. Being married now has taught me a lot. There are no more packing parties. When you are married, it is constant work. If you want it to work, you must do the work required. The biggest advice that I could give to anyone about anything is, pray about it. There is power in a praying woman. There is power in a praying man. There is power in prayer, period! Prayer is the solution to all of our problems. I used to tell Brandon, "either you can stand up and be the man that I need, or sit down so the next man can". He was able to do both, and I never realized that him doing both would lead us to where we are now. He sat and got himself together. He got his life in order, and took the steps that he needed to take to get himself right for him first, and then me. He then, took a stand to come back for what was his all along, me. This is true love. Our love story kind of reminds me of the movie "The Notebook". This movie is one of the greatest love stories of all times in my eyes, other than ours. There are a few correlations in this movie to our story. One of the main one's is, Noah getting the house prepared in hopes that Allie would come back. He had faith in his preparation that one-day she would return, although she did not seem to have planned to do so. Furthermore he got the house that she said that she wanted. Brandon is my Noah and I am his Allie. He prepared his home for his wife, and got the house that I dreamed would be our first home. Before I moved in, it was just a house. He even said that it didn't feel like home until I came in and added my scent to it. Home is where the heart is. He has told me on several occasions, "Ki, you made this house a home". Allie never felt like she could be herself with the guy she was planning to marry, she loved to paint, and never did around him. He did not even know that she liked to paint. There were things that I really enjoyed doing but did not ever do with or around Peter. He never really got a chance to know me, which isn't such a bad thing. When Allie returned to Noah, she never looked back. When I returned to Brandon, I never looked back. I love him more now than I ever have before. He put in the work needed to get me back. Sometimes when you are hurt, it just seems like it is never going to get any better, but it does. I will be the first to say, and I am sure Brandon could back me up on this, but it is hard to sleep with a broken heart. Have you ever tried to sleep with a broken heart? Doesn't it just ache more at night? It is almost like you gasp for your soul versus air to breathe. The thought of that person not coming back is just unsettling. They say it is one thing to mourn over a person that is never coming back because they have passed away, but it is another thing to mourn for a person that is still alive. Both are very painful and indescribable. True love isn't just about the ups, it's about the downs too. But, the best true love is when the ups outweigh the downs. The best relationship advice I could give you is one that our pastor gave us in our marriage counseling, which we took after getting married. We thought that even though we had just gotten married, we still wanted to be equipped with the proper tools to fight for our marriage when things got a little tough. The pastor made a chart of withdrawals and deposits. He asked us questions and the answer to those questions went in to one of the two "love banks". At the end when we saw that our deposit side was much more than the withdrawal side, he confirmed that love bank was being more poured into than drained. It is not healthy to be with people that drain you. People that constantly take, take, take. When you are with people that constantly take from you, you can look up and be left with nothing. When I say fight for what you love or with who you love, I do mean with a smart mind. Don't be with a Peter that is constantly draining you and think that it is your sign to "fight". That is your sign to take "flight". Those relationships are completely unhealthy. Peters are taking way more than giving. Peters come with too much weight, he is going to weigh you down. Don't get me wrong, love is amazing, when it is with the right person. But, don't waste your time loving the wrong person. You can do bad all by yourself. Don't be the "lingering" friend like me. Drop that dead weight and work on you. Love is blind, I know it's cliché, but it is true. Don't be so blind that you mistake red flags for flaws. It is important to know when to walk away or when to fight for love. My grandmother has always said, "you never really know people, you only know of them". Basically, you never know what a person is capable of doing, so don't be surprised when they do things to hurt you. I thank God for the people that he had in place in my life to help me get out of what may have potentially been a dangerous situation. When my friend Amy called me with that wake up call that is what I needed to snap out of something that was not for me. That one call completely changed my life.

There are so many people out there that miss the signs that God place right in their faces. The signs for me were there over and over again, but God needed to let me know in a way that I knew it was coming directly from him. God used Amy to give me the message I needed. Leaving that toxic relationship with Peter was very scary because I did not know if the threats he was making were real. My anxiety attacks came often when I first left him alone from the thought of him coming back to harm me. I knew that God had me covered though so I didn't worry too much. With guys like Peter, they are victimizers, once they are forced to move on from one victim, they move on to the next. More of his mess came out once I left him and I couldn't do anything but thank God over and over again for saving me. I got a call from one of my best friends as I was pulling up to my house. She just so happened to be talking to one of her co-workers, and somehow in the conversation they found out that they both knew Peter. She was one of his cousins. My friend told her about the crazy relationship we had and how I had to leave him alone, she also mentioned that he had a lot of kids and that was a lot to deal with. She said, "oh, my best-friend used to deal with him, but she left him alone. She found out that he had six or seven kids". She told me after that the lady started to crack up and said that everyone was messing with her cousin, and that he had a lot of women. She also asked was I the "tall girl" that he was with at his moms funeral. I am 5'2, no one can mistake me for being tall. When she told me that, I knew exactly who she was speaking of as I flashed back to the day of the funeral. I remember leaving out the door before heading to the burial, and he was standing there with some tall girl that had her arm around him. I did not think anything of it because, we were at a funeral, and I just assumed that she was family. Initially my gut was telling me it was something to that, but I completely ignored it because of the circumstances. Come to find out that woman was another woman that he was dealing with. He had some slick ways of doing things. I didn't play it back in my head until later, but even his "uber" rides were suspect. He always rode in the front seat, this was a cover up move too. If someone were to see him in the car with another woman, all he had to say was it was an uber, because I knew that he always sat in the front. Anyway, once my friend explained the situation of him having 6 or 7 kids, she said the cousin started laughing and said, "Six or seven. Girl how about he has NINE kids. Oh, but when you count the set of twins that he just had, that would make ELEVEN"!! When she told me that, my stomach hit the floor. ELEVEN KIDS? WTF! One of my girlfriends referred to him as a "stop and dump", meaning he would just get with women, get them pregnant and leave them. Now, when my best friend told me this news, it wasn't completely new to me. When we were together, he called me and told me that one of his friends cheated on his girlfriend, got the girl pregnant and she was having twins. My response to what he told me was irate. I kept saying, "Why would he do that to her! Cheating is wrong, period. But, to cheat and actually have a baby on the way? That is a constant reminder! And TWINS to top it off? OMG, that is crazy". His response was, "I know right, don't tell anyone I told you that". After he told me I would ask him about the friend and the twins to see if they had been born yet or just to get a status update, and he would say that he did not know. I stopped asking after a while because he wasn't getting any updates, so I thought. How slick was he? The entire time he was talking about himself getting someone pregnant with twins. If that isn't a snake move, I don't know what is. He was trying to protect his lie so that if it ever got back to me, I would defend him by saying that someone got him mixed up with his friend. "No, it is his friend that had the twins, not him", I told my girlfriend. She said, "No, Rickia. The twins are his, I just talked to his blood cousin and that woman knew for sure". Hearing that made me sick to my stomach at the thought that he even was playing with my life like that. She continued on by saying that she was so happy that Brandon and I were back together. She said it best about Peter, "he was just enough to catch Brandon's attention and get himself together, but also he was just enough for Brandon to be able to get you back". Real talk that was the truth. He was enough, but not enough. I don't know how many times I thanked God that night. I was so thankful that he removed me just in time, just in enough time for me not to have to go home to that fool and deal with THAT! It all made even more sense. Him being gone for days and not really calling me, was an indication that he was with someone else. When a man isn't coming around or home for days at a time, please believe he has somewhere to stay. All of the times that he would ignore my calls, and not read my texts until 5 a.m., (I guess when whoever he was with wasn't around) all made sense. When Brandon and I first got back together before getting married, one of the very first steps that we took was going to get tested together. This was the scariest time getting tested in my life. It was also the scariest time for Brandon getting tested. I went first, and got my results of being negative, then he came out with his negative results. This was a huge sigh of relief. I kept thinking about the Tyler Perry movie, Temptations. In that movie, there was a girl name Jude that got caught in a crazy, abusive relationship after leaving a man that was good for her. She later found out that he gave her HIV, and by then it was too late for her to try to patch things up with her ex. That story of Jude is the reality for many people. Again, this was God's mercy on BOTH Brandon and I. Peter had mentioned a few times on the calls he made to make arrangements to get his things that he needed to talk to me about something. He knew that him saying, "we need to have a serious talk" would trigger my anxiety. He insisted on meeting up with me, it was no way in h3ll that that was happening and I made sure to let him know that. His response was "well, you will find out later, just go to the doctor and get tested". A straight manipulator, he was a mass manipulator. Manipulation is also emotional blackmail. He wanted to see me in exchange of a conversation that he thought would be urgent to me. I was not going to meet him, but I was going to make sure that Brandon and I were both good before moving any further. Getting those negative results were like getting the golden ticket. After we got married and my birthday came around, it was time for my yearly physical. I knew that everything would come back good. I wasn't the least bit worried. I took my husband with me so that he could meet my new doctor. We gave her our entire background story and she was in tears when we got to the surprise wedding. I explained to her that I had nothing to hide and I wanted her to check for everything. I also wanted him to become a new patient of hers so that we could all share the same doctor. When we left her office, we went to the front desk to check out. "We will call you if there is anything wrong", when they said that line I said, "Ok"! I told them to make sure they checked me for EVERYTHING! Two weeks went by and there was no call, "whew thank God for that", I said to myself. I was on the phone with my mother when my phone rang on the other end, the caller ID read my doctors name. My heart dropped and I immediately went into a full panic attack. I was shaking, sweating and jittery. It was so bad that I had to connect my mother on 3-way to talk to the lady on the phone. They would not tell me what was going on over the phone let alone her. But, my mother has a way of talking to people to get some type of answer. The woman was still not able to tell her what it was, but she was able to confirm that it wasn't anything life threating. I caught the end of the conversation, because I had put the phone down when I started to lose my mind and crying in the middle of the street. Knowing that it wasn't life threatening eased my mind a lot. Everything was going so well, I was a new wife, business was starting to pick up, and everything was finally looking up. Everything had been restored. Now, this? I rescheduled some clients from the next day so that I could go get whatever news they wanted to deliver. I am a big baby when it comes to certain things, so I picked my mom up to go with me. I was still scared. When we got in the back the doctor asked if I wanted my mother in the room when she gave me my results. I told her that I had no problem with that because I was going to tell her anyway. My doctor causally said, "its nothing serious. You just have trich. I am going to write you a prescription and send you on your way. Your husband can get his filled as well". Wait, wait, wait slow down, what the heck is "trich"? I had no idea what it was, so I asked her and when she explained, it all clicked. The correct term is, "trichomoniasis". I had never heard of it until that day. I reflected on the day that I thought I had a yeast infection when Brandon and I first got together, it later went away, so I thought. I called Brandon and delivered the news to him. The best part of this was that no one was mad or upset. We had just gotten back together from both dealing with other people. There was no one to blame because neither one of us would ever be able to tell who it came from. We were both happy that it wasn't anything life threatening and that we could FINALLY move on from ALL of the past. Whew, I am exhausted from reflecting on all the pain, hurt and drama that I have endured. The weight of the past was still on the both of us, but after that doctor's scare, we were both able to finally cut the ties of anything that was from our past. I was so happy to finally have Peter and his lies out of my life, I didn't know WHAT to do. Oh yeah, that baby that he claimed to never be his, just so happened to be his "all of a sudden". I knew it! I guess once I left him alone he decided that he wanted to claim the baby. Maybe he needed a place to stay and he was trying to get in good with the mom, who knows. It was just so ironic that he popped up on my cousin's instagram timeline holding the baby that he said was never his, as soon as he realized that I was done with him. God showed us his mercy over and over and over again. We needed a vacation after that. It was time that we truly enjoy our new life and new marriage together. Next trip up was Mexico. Our trip to Mexico was amazing. We had the time of our lives. This was like our second honeymoon. We went to Mexico for "our" birthday in July. We always celebrate our birthdays together because they are exactly two months apart. So, if we take a trip in May, June or July, it is still considered one birthday trip. In Mexico we had an amazing time. It is so funny how life works. Just a year before that trip, Brandon called me complaining about how he did not want to go on a trip to Mexico (with whomever he was speaking of) for his birthday. He complained about the trip to me up until the day that he went and even when he got back. He kept saying, "I do NOT want to go. I'm going to go though, but I swear I can't wait to get back and I haven't even left". A whole year later, he reminded me of that time, and there WE were in Mexico having the time of our lives. We could not wait to go and we were not at all anxious to get back. We partied, loved on one another, went on amazing excursions, and ate amazing food. Oh yeah and we shopped! One night we were on the water at a very nice restaurant and he blessed the food before we ate. He always blesses the food for us. As he thanked God for the food, I saw him getting choked up and he started to cry and said, "God thank you for my wife. Thank you for sending her back to me" and he hurried and rushed to say Amen to control his tears. God is so good! He made us new! "Who wants that perfect love story anyway, cliché".

10 FINAL LOOK

AS I LOOK BACK OVER MY LIFE

Although I have bottled my emotions up most of my life, and masked a lot of my pain, writing this book has truly been therapeutic. This book was the perfect place for me to let it all out. It is important to create a space to let it all out, whether that is to a friend, therapy, meditation, journaling, or writing a book. It is beneficial to me in the servicing industry to mask my emotions. If you don't master the art of controlling your emotions when you are in the servicing industry, you will hurt your business. I have been emotionally dysfunctional from everything that has hurt me in my life. This dysfunction has spilled into many other areas in my life and made many negative and positive impacts. I have struggled with telling people how I feel, I usually show them. When I love a person, I keep them close and would do anything for them. When a person crosses me, I distance myself from them, many times without warning. I have not always been good at receiving love. I am great at showing it by giving my all to people that I love. Most of my life I have operated with an emotional disconnect. I haven't always adapted to change well. I like structure and the consistency of knowing what I am getting out of life, relationships, and friendships. This even trickles over into my eating habits, when I go out to eat, I often get the same thing that I am used to at every restaurant. It is rare that I try anything too new with food. Me not having control over things have triggered me to have anxiety. Sometimes me trying to control my emotions may hurt others. When people cry, I am not the best responder. I do not know what to say or do. Many times, I have ignored a person crying, if they aren't looking for me for a response. This is me thinking that, maybe they don't want me to know they are crying. Some people, like me, like to just cry in peace. Others that are not like me may simply need a hug. I do not like to be seen crying or really even held too much while I am crying because it makes me feel uncomfortable once the tears have dried. People never know how I am really feeling when things bother me, because I have a habit of walking away with no explanation. When I was in college, I had a job working as a staff assistant and I worked there for about 6 months to a year. I got fired, and never mentioned to anyone what was going on. They literally told me about 2 hours before it was time for me to leave. I left that day as if they were going to see me the next day. I said, "see ya'll later", some of the responses were, "ok, see you tomorrow". I never corrected them, I just let them think that I would be back to work the next day. I was angry about losing my job and did not want to deal with the emotions of that by having to explain it to people. I have always had my guard up to protect myself from getting hurt. Many times it backfired, because when I would finally let my guard down, I always got hurt in some shape or form. My biggest relationship issues have been my communication. If I feel that I am being attacked with words, I completely shut down. I will block numbers, turn my phone off, or if it is a situation where I would have to see the person, I would completely ignore their presence. Thank God that the positive has truly outweighed the negative in my life. I over love on the people closets to me. I would truly hand them the world if I could. My children are loved abundantly, I constantly kiss on them and tell them how much I love them every single day. I leave an open door of communication with them. I pay attention to their moods, and patterns. If I notice that they aren't their normal selves, I sit and talk with them. I ask them what is wrong until I get answers. I always want them to be able to express how they feel, because I want them to know how to cope with their feelings. Because of this, my daughter is very transparent with expressing how and why she feels the way that she feels. Because my mother wasn't always there, I don't miss a beat in my kid's lives'. I make sure that I am able to be at every major event that they have, this is the luxury that I enjoy the most about being self-employed. I am that friend that gives some of the best advice and the biggest listening ear. I am an over nurturer, well, in my world there is no such thing as being too nurturing. I even treat my husband like a big baby, after all men aren't anything but big babies anyway. As soon as he has the slightest discomfort, he calls me and I come running with my nurse/wife hat on. I am very careful with my words, even when I am angry. I try not to say anything that will stick to a person as things have stuck to me. Most of my emotional dysfunctions are coping mechanisms for me, it is really me just trying to protect myself. My anxiety may have triggered from not being able to cope with my emotions as well. I can't thank God enough for delivering me from all of the adversities that I have faced. As I stated before, my biggest prayer is for God to put me in a position to be able to help others. Me telling you my deepest secrets is never what I imagined, but I had to let out my hurt, pain and adversities that I have faced in order to free myself. Writing this book took me on an emotional rollercoaster. I cried, smiled, and laughed through the entire process. I am finally at a place where I know who I am. I am a confident woman and I know who and what deserves to be in my presence. With all of the hurt and pain that I dealt with, I managed to overcome it. There were many hurtful things said and done to me in the past, I do not hold anyone hostage of their actions. I thank God we are all in a great space now. Now is what matters. I am sure that I have said or done hurtful things as well to others and I apologize for any pain that I have ever caused anyone. There are people that will say and do things to knock you off your game, but you must keep going. Life is short, if you have a dream, go pursue that dream. I am serving my purpose in life. It took me years to figure out what my purpose was in life. I finally figured out that helping people makes me happy. Doing hair and even writing this book is helping someone. I get so much joy out of helping others. Every day that I go to work, I leave knowing that I was able to help people. Hair is the start of so many things. Confidence starts at your head. When your hair is done, you immediately feel better. People land jobs because they stepped in an interview with confidence that they gained from their hair. The right hair do will have you leave a toxic relationship. As I reflect back, many of those days that I was dealing with some of the things I discussed, my hair was not done. I was looking exactly how I felt, a mess. I'm sure my hair was done when I finally decided to leave LOL. But in all seriousness, you have to know your worth and what you deserve. My clients have seemed to have the best seats in the building when they come get their hair done. It is all about them, it is their "me" time where they can just relax and vent. I am the open ear, shoulder to cry on, and therapist to give advice. It feels good to be able to be the client for a chance. Today, you know more about me than anyone has ever known. I went into this being very transparent. They say that God blesses you for being obedient. When I first started writing this book, I was not being obedient, I just wanted to say what I wanted people to know. I was too embarrassed to talk about some of the things that I had been through. I am the co-author of this book, God is the writer, trust me he is, I would have NEVER said most of the things in this book on my own. Everything that I said, he wanted me to say, it is not about me. It is about helping the people that HE called me to help. Every time that I sat to write, I prayed that he would give me the words and things to say that he wanted me to say. God is simply using me as the vehicle to deliver you my testimony. If it was up to me? I would have tip toed on every person that I loved feelings and that would have affected the impact of this book. Some of those people hurt me, some helped me, and some did both. But in the end, every person that was ever connected to me in this book, helped lead me to my amazing testimony. I could have lost my life from toxic relationships. Harsh words could have made me feel like a failure and never want to succeed. My parents not being there when I needed them could have pushed me into looking for love in all the wrong places. I never looked for love in the wrong places, the wrong love just so happened to find me. But, God. That is a complete sentence! I thank him for 2nd and 3rd and 4th chances!! I felt so heavy writing this book and as it is coming to a close, I feel light as a feather. I got everything out in this book. I wouldn't use social media as a platform to air out my dirty laundry. There is a time and place for everything; now is the time, and this book is the place. I am so grateful for where I am in life right now. I have peace, you can never put a price on your peace. I wanted people to get to know me outside of social media. Social media is the world where everyone portrays their life to be a certain way, and I can't say that I blame them. It's not really the place for me to blast my business. But, outside of me being a woman of God, wife, mom and business owner, I have so many other layers. When Brandon and I got back together, I posted a picture and briefly talked about us breaking up and getting back together. That one brief post got so much good feed back, people were inspired. But, they only knew the surface, not just how ugly it was before it got to be beautiful. People can't always relate to perfection. Some people need to hear that your life has been or is just as effed up as theirs is or has been. I am sure there have been plenty of whispers about my life, but now you get to hear it from the horse's mouth. It's a difference when you can own up to your mess, it's like freeing yourself from people using your pain as a weapon against you. It no longer hurts. I have truly grown through all that I had to go through. God is not done with me, he is just getting started. He is about to do some things in my life that I would never imagine and I can feel the shift in the atmosphere. A few years ago, I took a class and I paid over $1,000 to take it. I had no idea what made me sign up for the class, or even what it was about. But, I took it because I really liked the lady that was teaching the class. I had been watching her on instagram, I loved her work, and I loved her personality. Being in her presence in the class alone was inspiring. She was everything that I wanted to be as a successful hairstylist. While we were in the middle of class, she stopped and said that God had just spoken to her. I remember her words so vividly. She said, "Wow, I have to say something that God has placed on my heart. You are going to be so successful! God is going to do some things in your life that are going to blow your mind. Once you break out of that shell, he is going to move you in ways that you could never imagine. You can't even imagine how successful you are going to be. I can feel your ambition all the way from here and you aren't even saying anything". When she initially said "you" she had to say it twice because I had no idea that she was talking about me. She pointed little ole me out in a room full of people. I never went back to take my test for that class to get certified, but I am convinced that my entire purpose of going was to get a message from God that he placed in her to convey to me. Her words stuck with me ever since. Anytime that I have doubted myself I reflect on what she said, and I reminded myself that God had some really amazing things in store for me. I just thank him for trusting me to be a deliverer to help with someone else's deliverance. You may be reading this book for one of these reasons: you love and support me, you saw someone talking about it, you want to be inspired, you want a story or someone you can relate to, you wanted to see if you were in it, or your nosey. Whatever the reason was, guess what? The challenge I made earlier for you to put your phone down, I already got you there, and I impacted you in some way. You put your phone down to read this book. I want to encourage you to keep pushing. Get ride of anything or anyone toxic in your life. Verbal abuse is very real and can cause you to lose yourself in hurtful words. Anxiety doesn't always need medicine to cure it, sometimes all the medicine you need is God and silence. God told me that it was time that I be quite and to listen to his instructions over my life. You may not have had the perfect upbringing, but don't use that as an excuse to your shortcomings. You are in control of the life that you want to live. Life is meant to be abundant in all areas. Tomorrow is not promised, you deserve happiness and peace, and these two things should never be up for compromising. I have compromised these very important things over and over again, but those days are over. Never compare your life to others. If it can happen for them, it can happen for you, but all in God's timing. Through me and Brandon's relationship, I saw what I wanted happening for everyone around me. Envy isn't the cure. I have mastered being completely happy for others, and in doing so I have been blessed so much. When you are genuinely happy for others, it's like that happiness comes back for you like a boomer-rang affect. In a world of social media pictures and status, it is easy to find yourself unhappy for others, really this is a reflection of you being unhappy with yourself. You can't possibly be unhappy for others when you are happy with yourself. Jealousy is a disease and it is diagnosed by you feeling a certain way about your own shortcomings. Jealousy is self-inflicted. Many times we want the lives of others because of how it looks from the outside looking in, but we never think about what a person went through to get to where they are.

Some of the people that we look up to the most have faced the most adversities. Your whole life can scroll by in the midst of you scrolling on social media and comparing your life to others. As a hairstylist, I have struggled with many things while standing behind the chair relationship issues, self issues, anxiety issues, health issues, and just whatever else life decided to throw at me. But, those things don't define me. I love who I am becoming. I am no longer who I was.

Allow me to reintroduce myself:

My name is Rickia Brown,

I am a God fearing woman, dedicated wife, mom and business owner. I believe that God can turn any and everything around. He can make old things new, the poor rich, the bad good, and the unimaginable reality. He comes first in my life. Can't no one move me like God. Ever since I started to put him first in my life, he has been showing up and showing out like none other. I amazed at the way that he is moving things in my life. He protects me, for no weapon formed against me shall prosper. He called me to the forefront to give my testimony and I thank him for seeing me trustworthy. My life is much different now. It is so much better. Today, I am free of anxiety. Everyday I feel good. Everything that I touch will turn to gold, and he has not even begun to work on all that he has planned for me. I thank you for taking the time out to ready this book and I pray that it inspires or helps you in plenty of ways. I am finishing this book empty. I truly gave you my all, the good, the bad, and the ugly. I am free. My hurt no longer holds me hostage. If he can do it for me, he can sure do it for you. Faith is taking the first step even when you can't see the next step.

Letter to my husband.

Dear Husband,

I thank you for being my number one fan and always having my back. I could never put into words the way that I feel about you. My love for you is unconditional. I thank you for your blessing on giving me the green light to tell my truths about our relationship. You giving me your blessing allowed me to feel that I could be completely transparent. It is your love that pushes me everyday. You came into my life and showed me what I did and what I did not want in a husband. You showed me qualities that I did not ever want in a man, yet you turned that around and set the best example of all the qualities that I do want in a man. Neither one of us are perfect. Marriage is constant work and everyday I thank God that I am able to work on it with you. You truly adore me and love me in a way that makes others love the way you love me. I thank you for listening to me and giving me all that I deserve. You are truly my best friend and I feel free knowing that I can completely be myself around you. Today we stand stronger than ever before. I thank you for standing in braveness with me in writing this book.

Love,

Your Wife

ABOUT THE AUTHOR

Rickia Brown is a Washington, D.C. native. She is the owner of Pretty Hair Rockz hair salon where she isn't just your hairstylist, she is also your counselor and friend. She loves to connect with people in ways that they are able to take something positive from her with them. There are many great things in the future coming up for Rickia. She is getting ready to launch her first podcast and mentorship program. Stay tuned for details by staying connected with her journey at:

www.prettyhairrockz.com

instagram: @prettyhairrockz

Subscribe to her website so that she can stay connected with you via email.

Made in the USA
Middletown, DE
07 December 2019